M000158366

Managing Millennials

Managing Millennials

The Ultimate Handbook for Productivity, Profitability, and Professionalism

Kevin E. Phillips

Routledge
Taylor & Francis Group

A PRODUCTIVITY PRESS BOOK

First published 2019
by Routledge
2 Park Square, Milton Park, Abingdon, Oxon OX14 4RN

and by Routledge
711 Third Avenue, New York, NY 10017

Routledge is an imprint of the Taylor & Francis Group, an informa business

British Library Cataloguing in Publication Data
A catalogue record for this book is available from the British Library

Library of Congress Cataloging in Publication Data
A catalogue record for this book is available from the Library of Congress

ISBN: 978-1-1384-8342-2 (hbk)
ISBN: 978-1-3510-5494-2 (ebk)

Typeset in Minion Pro
by Taylor & Francis Books

Contents

SECTION IV Making Changes, Taking Action

Foreword

"What should I do to motivate Michael?" "Lisa has so much potential, but I can't figure out how to get her to do more."

With over 40 years in business, I've frequently heard managers complain about individuals, and we'd work together to come up with solutions to improve performance—or let the challenging employee go. And if that one person's issues weren't addressed and she ended up underperforming, it usually wasn't that big of a deal to the company's overall performance.

Things are different today. Now when I am advising leaders across various industries, I am hearing from them all: "What can we do about these Millennials?" Now we are talking about a whole generation that is causing managers concern. It just seems so much harder than before, when we only had to deal with one person at a time. We don't have the option of ignoring this group—it is a critical mass. They are not only significant part of our current workforce, they are the future leaders of our organizations. The reality is, most businesses have little choice but to hire Millennials—and that is a good thing, once we figure out how to capitalize on all their strengths. Discounting the importance of figuring out how to get the best out of them will only lead to continued frustration—and ultimately corrode business results.

Some managers don't care—they see the problem as a new cohort of employees that must learn to grow up, and those managers keep managing the way they have in the past. These are the managers experiencing turnover or less-than-stellar performance. But many leaders recognize that this group is their future and the organization better figure out fast how to adapt to their new workforce. They read about Millennials, and may try to incorporate new management practices in a one-size-fits-all manner. Often, they are choosing the wrong practices to change, or they fail to see that Millennials are still individuals with different needs, personalities, and motivations.

In *Managing Millennials: The Ultimate Handbook for Productivity, Profitability, and Professionalism*, Kevin E. Phillips helps us see that yes, Millennials as a group have some unique characteristics, but they are not all uniform. I was amazed, as I read about the different characteristics of the subsets of this age group, I could identify people I knew in each category.

When figuring out how to manage differently, we need to look at how Millennials as a group are different from previous generations and also how they are individuals who deserve individual awareness, rather than painting everyone with the same brush. I am reminded of the change to the Golden Rule that I used to teach:

It is NOT: Do unto others as you would have them do unto you.
It IS: Do unto others as they want to be done unto.

The conundrum leaders face is figuring out how Millennials "want to be done unto." This book is a great tool for helping to learn the fundamentals.

Will changing management practices to encourage Millennials negatively affect the rest of the work force? Kevin provides a solid analysis of how Millennials differ from Baby Boomers and Gen Xers, and offers solutions for integrating them all into the workforce. As this new generation takes over leadership roles, this will be increasingly important to understand and manage.

Most of the leaders I work with truly care about people, and *all* of them care about business results. (OK, some managers only care about themselves, but they are not the type of people who are my clients—and they certainly don't invest in books like this.) In trying to drive increased profitability and returns in this business environment, leaders know they must make substantive shifts in their organization. They need more agility, fewer silos, and more cross-functional teamwork to get and stay ahead of the competition. It is remarkable how these solid business practices, necessary in the new millennium, are also indispensable in motivating Millennials. Kevin provides an excellent analysis of how these essential results-driven changes in running a business also have a direct positive effect on connecting with Millennials—creating even more incentive to examine how we can manage differently for improved productivity.

As long as I've known Kevin, he has been a "get it done" kind of person. Theories and debates are fine, but what can we do *now* to start making an impact? In this book, he provides practical steps to address specific problems. I believe these practical steps are what set this book apart. Once managers understand the framework, they can start implementing changes. Some changes may be small steps in their daily interactions and some may be larger organization-wide transformations, but all of them will have an impact.

Kevin has always had a knack for connecting with people, and he has an uncanny ability to ensure everyone is engaged. Lucky for the rest of us, he has shared his enthusiasm for a positive culture with his solid research, so we can all learn to be more effective. His writing reflects his passion to make the work environment a place where everyone thrives, is engaged in what they are doing, and ultimately leads to a healthy business. His first book, *Employee LEAPS: Leveraging Engagement by Applying Positive Strategies,* was another practical guide to optimizing performance by engaging employees to improve productivity and results. *Managing Millennials: The Ultimate Handbook for Productivity, Profitability, and Professionalism* takes engagement one step further by focusing on a key, and often misunderstood, subset of the workforce.

Enjoy the read—then make it work for you!

Elaine Kramer
*Retired Vice-President of Training and Leadership
Development, Pulte Homes
Owner, Kramer Organization, Organizational
Development Consultants*

Acknowledgments

I am beyond grateful for all the support, encouragement, and inspiration I have received throughout the development of this book. Specifically, thank you to my family and friends. Your love, kindness, patience, and compassion have inspired me.

I would like to especially thank Mike and Jill Phillips. There are truly no words; you have always been and always will be my mentors and voices of reason. I cannot count the number of times you have provided guidance, given support, or pushed me forward throughout the years. I will always be indebted to you for this. Joe and Lauren Phillips, thank you for being an extraordinary source of motivation, encouragement, and kindness. You have inspired me to strive for excellence and been a quiet voice that has encouraged me to pursue my goals.

Saul and Katy Chafin, and Dave and Beth Phillips, your unwavering love and support is beyond anything I could ever ask for. You truly are the foundation that has enabled me to pursue my dreams. Thank you also for being my editors and sounding board. Your continued support in my writing means the world to me!

Elaine Kramer, this book came together because of your insights, analysis, and ideas. You truly went above and beyond. Thank you for investing so much of your time and talents in this book.

Patrick Schneider, Sarah Custer, and Brian Ansley, thank you for giving so much of yourselves to make me a better person. You have endlessly poured into me with exceptional grace and selflessness. I am blessed for the friendships I share with each of you.

My 15 (not-so-little) nieces and nephews—Riley, Trent, Claire, Troy, Kaitlyn, Colton, Avery, Grant, Grey, Wesley, Kyle, Kayla, Jett, Spencer, and Sarah—thank you for bringing so much happiness into my life. You have always provided me so much joy and love. I hope my writing, in some form or fashion, creates a more fulfilling workplace for you.

ACS Quality Department, you are the work family I never knew I wanted. You make me smile every day, help me appreciate the little things in the office, and enable me to see why this work is so important. I value the friendships I have with each and every one of you.

Finally, Productivity Press, and more specifically, Michael Sinocchi, thank you for taking a chance on me and helping me bring this book to life. I am honored that you were willing to take on this project.

Author

Kevin E. Phillips is a 2017 Top 40 Under 40 Military Honoree, MBA graduate of the University of Michigan's Ross School of Business, advisor at CVS Health, United States Air Force Veteran, Center for Positive Organizations Fellow, project management professional, and independent consultant for entrepreneurs. For the past 15 years, he has worked in various business industries and organizations serving as a conduit between managers and Millennials, and knows exactly what it takes to increase motivation, unleash talent, and transform potential into productivity. This enables leaders to get to the root of problems quicker and discover solutions more efficiently, leading to better business results.

Introduction

Productivity, profitability, and professionalism are attributes every organization desires. They are characteristics that enable companies to reach their goals, become successful, and thrive! While there are certain formulas that have enabled businesses to reach these coveted objectives, throughout time the recipe for success continually changes. This can partly be attributed to the world changing, and more specifically, people changing.

Every generation brings with them unique experiences, different points of view, and new ways of thinking, and Millennials are no different; they think, act, and work differently than their predecessors. This changes the landscape of the corporate world while simultaneously requiring leaders to adapt their management style. This is not a new challenge: there has always been and will always be a culture clash when a new generation comes into the workforce.[1] This is because every employee group has idiosyncrasies that make them distinct.

So, while a manager may have led people for their entire career, their method of managing in the present day could be ill advised. Outdated approaches toward management do not deliver success with this new breed of employee. Rather than getting the best out of Millennials, their ability to perform is restricted. This is primarily because Millennials possess a unique perspective that does not fall in line with those who came before them. While there are certain characteristics of leadership that are important for every employee group, employee performance can vary considerably based on the way they are managed. This reality has become increasingly apparent with Millennials.

With over 55 million Millennials working in the United States today, the largest demographic in the workplace, they must be managed effectively if companies are going to succeed. Unfortunately, while this is widely accepted, many leaders fail to know what that looks like. They rely on past managerial experiences or use the Golden Rule as their guide. Though respectable in general, these approaches don't work. Millennials have different motivations, interests, and priorities, so can't be managed the same as their predecessors. This truth is reiterated throughout the entire book and is a primary reason so many companies are struggling with this generation.

Managing Millennials: The Ultimate Handbook for Productivity, Profitability, and Professionalism has been written to help leaders successfully manage Millennials by providing specific actions they can take to get the best out of this generation.

Managing Millennials has four sections. *Section I* is an introduction to the Millennial workforce and focuses on new challenges that have materialized because of Millennials entering the workplace. It highlights the values, interests, and passions Millennials have and shares the different ideologies and preferences that Millennials, Generation X, and Baby Boomers traditionally embrace for 12 important workplace topics. Section I ends with discussion on the 12 types of Millennial archetypes that are currently in the workforce. Areas of focus include their strengths and weaknesses, when they are at their worst, and how to get the best out of them.

Section II delves into the considerable changes that have taken place in the workforce and business world in recent years, and how they traditionally mirror one another. This section of the book enables the reader to gain a comprehensive understanding of how work environments and the way businesses operate are different than years past, and how you have to adapt to meet the needs of your employees and the market. The section ends with a case study on how Uber, Lyft, and Airbnb changed the landscape of their respective industries by breaking the mold, and effectively connects how inflexible companies and outdated management styles lead to the corrosion of successful businesses. This is evident from the way these companies disrupted their respective markets and how Millennials affect the workplace.

Section III shares unique information about Millennials and the work environment and is designed to encourage you to look beyond what has worked in the past. Areas of focus include little known secrets about Millennials and the importance of adapting your methodology to meet the demands of employees in this day's economy. The final chapter encourages readers to take an objective assessment of their department or organization to determine if certain Millennials should remain active with the organization or move on.

Finally, *Section IV* has over 100 ready-to-use solutions from 18 real-world issues that you can use to bolster productivity and get the best out of Millennials. The section has been separated into three distinct areas of focus: motivating Millennials, combining generations and producing results, and the good, the bad, and the ugly. This provides leaders the opportunity to target their specific challenging areas and select the solution that aligns best with their situation.

Managing Millennials: The Ultimate Handbook for Productivity, Profitability, and Professionalism will dramatically increase output and transform potential into productivity by helping leaders know exactly how to get the best out of Millennials. This book provides strategic insights, solutions, and direction that empower leaders to get into the hearts and minds of Millennials so that they can successfully communicate business priorities in a way that makes sense to this unique employee base. With that in mind, you are encouraged to use this book to get the best out of Millennials and transform your organization!

ENDNOTE

[1] C. Kadakia, *The Millennial Myth: Transforming Misunderstanding into Workplace Breakthroughs* (Oakland, CA: Berrett-Koehler, 2017), pp. 3–20.

Section I

Millennials in the Workplace

In 2002, a young high school student named Mark was chatting with friends when his computer suddenly stopped playing music because his playlist ended. Though not a big deal to most, Mark was frustrated because the music being played was nothing more than a list of songs generated exclusively by him. He believed there was a better way.

After mulling over potential solutions to his problem, he and a friend created a software program that learned about a listener's interests and ultimately recommended songs according to their taste. This enabled music to continue playing without the listener needing to manually upload songs, and with that, the Synapse Media Player was born.

The application was highly sought-after and could have generated considerable money for the high school senior. However, instead of selling it to a large IT company for a hefty profit, Mark released it at no charge knowing that more people would be able to access it that way. As a classic Millennial, he believed in serving the greater good rather than merely making a profit for himself. This young man went off to Harvard, where he eventually dropped out in lieu of another worthwhile opportunity, starting the revolutionary social media platform Facebook.

Long before Mark Zuckerberg made billions of dollars with his company, he was just a typical Millennial kid who enjoyed programming.

This made his decision to release Synapse to the public free of charge and choose university life rather than selling the program or going to work for one of the tech companies offering a hefty salary and great benefits confusing to many people. But to Mark, it all made sense. He was more interested in a college experience than a corporate job, autonomy instead of structure, and making a difference over making a buck.[1]

Looking back, Zuckerberg's decision to release his program free of charge did not derail his extraordinary success. Even if he had been just a typical Millennial who did not accumulate astonishing wealth, he would likely still have stood by the choice he made. He was interested in something that went far beyond merely making money.

****

This mentality is true for many Millennials. High salaries, bonuses, fringe benefits, and an elevated status in a company are all gratifying, yet in the end fail to capture the passions and interests of Millennials. Many leaders from other generations can't understand this mindset or cast it off as naïve. This causes them to become confused when their leadership fails to deliver the results that they expected.

Thinking from a holistic view, just as you are different than your predecessors, so too are Millennials different from you. This creates an inevitable clash of viewpoints, perspectives, and approaches toward work, while simultaneously creating clarity that it is not feasible to continue using the same approach toward management as you have in years past. To successfully manage Millennials, you must change your mindset and methodology.

Not surprisingly, each generation brings with it unique skills, assorted priorities, and alternative viewpoints that differ from its predecessors, and Millennials are no different. Millennials have a different lifestyle than previous generations did at the same age, and thus live their lives unlike their predecessors. The notion that managers will be able to successfully lead Millennials with a management style that worked in the past is inaccurate. There are a multitude of differences between the generations of yesteryear and Millennials, including social norms, lifestyle preferences, personal and professional goals, and overarching passions and interests. These differences are exacerbated with how the business world has changed. Focus on manual labor and mechanical skill has been replaced with automation and use of cognitive abilities. This further validates the fundamental need to manage employees differently.

This is often lost on leaders. Rather than work to understand the Millennial mindset and attempt to recognize the distinct areas in their lives that they value, many leaders instinctively typecast this generation while buying into the myths and rumors that they have heard. While there are Millennials who are poor performers and align closely to the stereotypes that have developed, these employees are typically the exception, not the rule. The majority of Millennials have a deep-rooted interest in working hard. The key is discovering the most effective way to manage them so that they can fulfill their role and deliver value to the organization.

ENDNOTE

[1] S. F. Brickman, Not-so-artificial intelligence, *The Crimson*, last modified October 23, 2003, http://www.thecrimson.com/article/2003/10/23/not-so-artificial-intelligence-for-his-high-school/.

1

The Millennial Challenge

Millennials are lazy, entitled, unreliable employees who were coddled by their parents, don't know how to work hard, and can't handle the real world. They come with too much emotional baggage, spend money on frivolous things, and are not willing to put forth effort on anything other than themselves.

There is no other explanation. The entire generation is a group of spoiled narcissists.

Or is there an alternative?

Could Millennials just be misunderstood? Could they have different values, interests, and passions that do not align with previous generations? Do their cognitive abilities eliminate the willingness to say "yes" to every order the boss gives because they are internally questioning whether they can fulfill their role more efficiently? And are they prioritizing their lives differently because they have a lifestyle that does not conform to a big house surrounded by a white picket fence, new car, and loving spouse with 2.5 kids?

Or could it be something different altogether?

Are a few Millennials in your office compelling you to stereotype everyone in this generation? Is the reckless behavior of a select group of Millennial celebrities on reality TV casting a negative shadow? Or is your preconceived mentality toward the work ethic of Millennials the cornerstone for your negative perspective?

Every generation has employees who range from uninspired and lacking motivation to dedicated and hardworking, so categorizing all Millennials as the same is misguided. However, there are a few overarching truths about Millennials that are causing challenges. Specifically, Millennials are different from every other generation in the workplace, leaders struggle to manage Millennials effectively, and businesses are placing emphasis on the wrong activities to motivate Millennials.

MILLENNIALS ARE DIFFERENT FROM EVERY OTHER GENERATION IN THE WORKPLACE

The values, interests, and passions that Millennials have do not align with previous generations, nor do they necessarily conform to what has been perceived as "right" by others. Millennials march to the beat of their own drum and would rather create a unique path than mindlessly follow the footsteps of their predecessors.

Unfortunately, managers from other generations do not always appreciate this reality, casting it off as an excuse for behavior that does not line up with the values, interests, and passions that they hold dear; it is merely justification for behavior that is less than virtuous. This disconnect shouldn't necessarily be a surprise. Every generation has gone through different social, economic, and cultural experiences during their formative years that have helped to define their perspective, spark their interest, and shape how they view the world. This makes it predictable that each generation approaches work with a keen methodology that does not always connect well with other employee groups. Instead, their wide-ranging philosophies and diverse viewpoints create a lack of congruence in the workplace. This is often the case with Millennials.

Millennials bring a new set of burdens that extend far beyond what the typical manager is accustomed to handling. This problem is intensified due to leaders not modifying their management style appropriately. This leads to less than optimal results.

Disappointingly, instead of accepting accountability for their efforts going awry, many in leadership believe the worker is the one who has failed. This generates various attitudes and viewpoints toward Millennials in the workplace that are less than flattering. While some of these perceptions could be true, many lack credibility. They are myths that have been created because of the lack of understanding a Millennial's perspective or approach toward work, and an unwillingness to accept that their values, interests, and passions do not align with what has been considered the norm.

Three of the most recurrent myths that follow Millennials are that they can't follow directions, they are needy, and they do not see their jobs as a priority. If one has ever dealt with difficult Millennials, it is very easy to accept these stereotypes as truth. However, when digging for a deeper understanding as to why Millennials are given these ill-advised designations, opinions often change.

Specifically, while in previous generations subordinates would follow a leader's direction (for better or worse) with minimal questioning, this is different in today's workplace. In many ways, Millennials are the most prepared generation coming into the workforce ever; they have more education, been exposed to more diverse experiences, and possess more access to information than any other group of employees. Because of this, it shouldn't be surprising that they are always asking the question, "Why?" Their cognitive skills are looking for a better way to complete a task and they are not content with the "We have always done it that way" mentality.

Additionally, while the perception of neediness could reign supreme when Millennials are peppering you with questions, it is not to bother you. Asking questions enables them to continuously improve while providing the opportunity to make adjustments to meet your demands. This ensures they will stay on course with every project.

Finally, the belief that Millennials do not see their jobs as a priority seems to be evident throughout every industry and organization. Everywhere you turn, there is some member of this generation that is pushing work aside because of a more attractive alternative. While it is true that some Millennials place emphasis on activities that will allow them to actively avoid doing their job (as do a subset of every generation), still other Millennials choose to fulfill their roles during times throughout the day that have not historically been considered work hours.

This is because they are highly mobile and capable of working anywhere they have an internet connection. While for previous generations it was imperative for employees to be in the office Monday through Friday from 9 to 5, a laptop and internet connection make that a thing of the past. This is why Millennials are comfortable taking a 2-hour lunch and leaving work at 4 p.m. to grab dinner with friends. They know that they will inevitably jump back online in the evening to complete their responsibilities. Though not possible with every role (e.g., customer-facing jobs, frontline supervisors, etc.), many positions no longer require employees to come into the workplace. This is hard for Baby Boomers and some members of Generation X to understand. Laptops weren't mainstream when these employees were growing up. Conversely, most Millennials can't remember a time without an internet connection everywhere they go, so plugging in at an offsite location is almost second nature.

There are many other myths beyond these three that are instrumental in the way Millennials are inaccurately perceived and incorrectly labeled. While a subset of Millennials is the reason these stereotypes have been created, it is irresponsible to label all of them as fitting the mold.

LEADERS STRUGGLE TO SUCCESSFULLY MANAGE MILLENNIALS

In a recent poll of more than one million U.S. workers, a bad boss or supervisor is the number one reason employees quit their job; not long work hours, poor pay, or failure to get a promotion, it is leadership.[1] Additionally, there are over 55 million Millennials working in the United States today and two-thirds of them are planning on leaving their current organization by the year 2020, while a quarter see themselves somewhere else in less than a year.[2] With Millennials expected to represent three-quarters of the workforce by 2025, this is extremely disconcerting.

Companies must adapt their management style to keep their Millennials or expect to see continued high rates of attrition that will cost them dearly. This is easier said than done. Millennials are unique, and though each generation has distinct characteristics that bring with them unique challenges, it seems that Millennials carry a new set of behavioral traits that are outside the norm for managers.

This problem is compounded due to managers not finding ways to get the best out of their people, but rather managing the same way they have in the past. By not capitalizing on the strengths of this new employee base, the opportunity for leaders to get the best out of their employees is eliminated. Many in leadership fail to recognize this and point at the worker who is not producing, instead of looking internally and determining if modifying their approach would deliver stronger returns on individual (and collective) performance.

More specifically, in the past money was seen as the ultimate motivator and served as the driver for increasing productivity. If you wanted employees to perform a certain way, you needed to increase their wage, and theoretically, the bigger the pay increase the better the results. Members of past generations would often jump at the chance to increase their salary and would do whatever was necessary to make more money. Even nominal increases in pay would lead to better performance.

While financial compensation is a motivator that can generate specific behavior in Millennials, small increases in pay will not provide a deeper level of commitment, it will only generate short-term compliance.[3] And though Millennials want to be provided an attractive wage and appreciate receiving a bump in salary when they deliver results, they would much prefer being given rewards that extend beyond their bank account. Time off, working from home, and being involved in important projects are all benefits that are valued over a small salary increase.

Unfortunately, many leaders do not appreciate this reality, casting it off as inaccurate or lacking rationale. This is primarily because it is so different from their mindset. Their dismissal of Millennial interests and failure to modify their approach toward managing this generation flagrantly pushes this subset of the workforce away from producing optimal results. Not capitalizing on what actually motivates Millennials causes organizations to lose valuable employees because of turnover. These problems are catastrophic and can cause organizations to falter when they should be flourishing.

BUSINESSES ARE PLACING EMPHASIS ON THE WRONG ACTIVITIES TO MOTIVATE MILLENNIALS

Many companies attempt to actively engage Millennials. As the up-and-coming generation that is continuing to make considerable impact in the business world, most organizations understand the necessity of embracing the Millennial employee and keeping them actively engaged. Unfortunately, quite often leaders are placing emphasis in the wrong areas. They attempt to stir up fresh energy and create an exciting environment by buying doughnuts for the staff every week, putting a gym in the office, or bringing in a ping-pong table for the break room.

These trendy ideas are interesting, but when thinking holistically, do they actually produce better business results? Are a dozen doughnuts really the only thing that is holding your team back from being productive? What percentage of employees use the gym in the office? And how many employees play ping-pong every day?

It is naïve to believe that these arbitrary activities are truly the bedrock for Millennials becoming more motivated to produce results. Instead, they are shortsighted solutions presented to appease employees for the interim—a mere Band-Aid designed to stop a gushing wound. It takes more than these trivial activities to captivate the Millennial workforce.

Nevertheless, leaders look at trendy businesses that highlight fun and exciting activities such as "Muffin Mondays" and team trivia contests or hip start-ups that seem to thrive on Friday happy hours and "bring your dog to work days," and try to emulate them. Though fun, these events do not get to the core of what an employee truly desires. They are merely activities that allow members to distract themselves from their work. In the end, they do not have considerable bearing on whether an employee is productive. So, while it may serve you well for the short-term, provide a boost of energy occasionally, and encourage members to work a little harder for a certain project, the arbitrary incentives do not deliver sustained increases in productivity.

To be successful, companies must do a better job of understanding Millennials so that they can place emphasis on activities that will inspire. The traditional Millennial is not one who is attracted to shiny objects or basic handouts that lack true value. They want to work for a company that makes a legitimate attempt at capturing their unique interests and places emphasis on what motivates them intrinsically. Everything else is irrelevant. Unfortunately, gaining awareness of the specific actions that will motivate Millennials is not always easy. Millennials will not typically express what motivates them at work, especially when their ideals fall outside the norm or do not align with the current culture of the organization. Regardless, it is imperative for companies to expand their ideology and for leaders to transform their mindset to successfully generate sustained Millennial productivity.

BRINGING IT ALL TOGETHER

Millennials are a new breed of employee that has great potential. Unfortunately, too often they are categorized as high-maintenance or problem employees before they ever get the chance to prove themselves. This is for a variety of reasons, but can often be attributed to a subset of their generation having less than desirable work habits or because they have different ideologies and preferences that do not align with their predecessors.

More specifically, instead of accepting that each Millennial brings unique skills, interests, and work habits to the office, the entire generation is lumped together and considered poor performers. They are labeled spoiled, self-focused, and not interested in putting forth an honest day's work. Serving as the perfect scapegoat, Millennials are branded as the problem instead of it being accepted that they simply do not fit into the preconceived belief of how employees should think, act, and work.

For companies to succeed, leaders must manage Millennials effectively. Already having the largest percentage of employees in the labor force, and growing each year, it is critical that buy-in from this generation materialize for companies to be successful. For this to occur, companies (and leaders) must embrace the changes that these employees bring to the workplace, modify management's approach, and capitalize on the strengths Millennials bring to the office.

ENDNOTES

[1] L. Oien, People quit their boss, not their job, *Business Paths*, last modified September 8, 2015, https://lead-succeed.com/news/people-quit-their-boss-not-their-job-4-keys-to-attracting-and-retaining-the-best-and-brightest/.

[2] S. Lebowitz, Here's a key reason why all of your Millennial employees are quitting, *Business Insider*, last modified January 17, 2016, http://www.businessinsider.com/why-millennial-employees-are-quitting-2016-1.

[3] K. Phillips, *Employee LEAPS: Leveraging Engagement by Applying Positive Strategies* (New York: Business Expert Press, 2016), p. 11.

2

Generational Diversity

Fax machines, dial-up internet, VCRs, and CD-ROMs all had their day in the sun, a time when they were valuable commodities that everyone wanted. If you were privileged enough to have any of these technologies at the time they were hot, you were considered to be on the cutting edge. Today stores no longer carry these items in stock because they are simply outdated.

Unfortunately, while most companies easily adapt to changes in the market, the same can't be said about how these same organizations manage their employees. Companies (and leaders) often remain steadfast about policies and procedures and how they manage their personnel. This inevitably stifles productivity.

For example, while in the past pay raises and moving up the corporate ladder were seen as the primary ways to motivate employees, this is not the case for Millennials. Millennial ideology centers less on finances and promotions, and more on intrinsic motivators and intangible benefits. Regrettably, many leaders, especially those who are not Millennials, do not grasp this concept, choosing instead to believe that Millennial productivity, satisfaction, and retention revolve around what they (the managers) deem to be important: money and advancement. This often leaves leadership lacking the basic understanding why certain management initiatives fail to yield the expected results.

Digging deeper, while many people have a good understanding of what encourages them personally and know what inspires friends and close colleagues, quite often individuals lack awareness of what is important to the majority of their team or department. It shouldn't be surprising that employees possess different workplace ideologies and preferences. Different cultures, ethnicities, social norms, personalities,

13

and behavioral traits that represent our workforce ensure that there is never a one-size-fits-all solution for ensuring people are engaged in their daily activities.

This is true for generational diversity as well. However, while various forms of diversity are frequently discussed, disparity among generational ideologies and preferences is often forgotten. This is a critical failure. Each employee group maintains different perspectives on a variety of matters in the workplace, and all believe their ideologies and preferences are the most suitable. These contrasting viewpoints provide a rationale for why companies are having so many problems blending generations.

While a lot of progress has been made, there is still a learning curve, making it no surprise that friction can run rampant when generations are combined. Because of this, it is important to gain a better understanding of the perspective of each employee group currently part of the labor force. Following are 12 important workplace topics, and customary ideologies and preferences that Millennials, Generation X, and Baby Boomers have for each.

MILLENNIALS—BORN 1980 TO 1999

1. *Mentality Toward Work*: Millennials work to live and are not interested in spending every waking moment on the job. Though they want to get ahead in their careers, they are interested in doing so on their terms, and that doesn't include working in the office from sunrise to sunset. They place high value on their social lives and do their best to avoid missing opportunities to enjoy life for work.

2. *What is Important*: Millennials are steadfast in believing that productivity and results should count for more than just being present. If they can fulfill their duties in less time than others, they should not be confined to the office or penalized for finishing their day. Further, because they believe employees should be evaluated based solely on productivity, not how, when, or where they get their work done, they believe they should be able to do their job wherever they are comfortable. It shouldn't matter if they are in the office, at home, or at a local coffeehouse.

3. *Rewarding Quality Performance*: Millennials are not as motivated by financial compensation as their predecessors. Though receiving a raise is appreciated, they would much rather have intangible benefits that extend beyond their bank account; time off, working from home, and being involved in important projects are all rewards that are valued.

4. *Leadership*: Millennials straddle the line between respecting authority and feeling that leadership is out of touch. Though many Millennials respect quality leadership, some are brazen enough to believe that they should be in charge. This varies for many reasons, but can often be attributed to the transformation of business operations due to technological advances that management doesn't always fully understand. Additionally, Millennials respond poorly to those who act in an authoritarian manner and/or expect to be revered simply because of positional power.

5. *Teamwork and Collaboration*: Millennials appreciate coming together as a team and thrive in a collaborative work environment. Though they are confident in their skills and appreciate the opportunity to personally bring value to the organization, they enjoy collaborative environments where they can use the talents and abilities of everyone.

6. *Sharing Information*: Millennials love having information so much that they have developed a fear of missing out (FOMO) if they are not included. Social media, smartphones, and constant contact with virtually anyone they want to communicate with at any time have instilled a deep desire to know everything that is going on. This has migrated into their professional lives.

7. *Communication Medium*: Though they are comfortable with all forms of communication, Millennials much prefer using technology such as email, IM, text, WebEx, etc., over face-to-face interaction. This enables them to communicate with whomever they want to at any time. However, there are still some circumstances in which they prefer face-to-face interaction: during emergencies and high turmoil situations, they want to have direct communication with leadership.

8. *Innovation*: Millennials value innovation and appreciate the opportunity to optimize workplace operations. They are interested in continually innovating and believe that it is the only way to stay

on top. They have an extreme bias for optimizing operations and see "business as status quo" as taking a step back.

9. *Technology*: Millennials believe technology is king and are interested in continually learning how to use new programs to enhance their skills; this does more than just add value to the company, it is a source of pride. Millennials love mastering new technology and appreciate how advances enable them to be flexible with how they fulfill their duties. Yet for all the benefits technology delivers, Millennials typically fail to recognize the financial implications that come with them. They do not appreciate the financial burden organizations must bear to acquire new tools, programs, or applications.

10. *Commitment to the Company*: While Millennials are not against having long-term relationships with employers, this is only true if it is on their own terms. They will change companies in an instant if there is an intriguing opportunity waiting for them. To keep Millennials for an extended period of time, companies must provide captivating work and opportunities to develop.

11. *Dress/Attire*: Millennials appreciate the opportunity to work in a casual environment where they don't need to dress up. This is why working remotely is so attractive to many; it eliminates the need to wear proper business attire.

12. *Intangibles*: Millennials are a new breed of employee. They love social media, multitasking, and technological advances, and expect to be treated with distinct value due to the unique skills that they possess. They also appreciate friendly, diverse environments, value corporate social responsibility, and believe that everyone should have a voice.

GENERATION X—BORN 1965 TO 1979

1. *Mentality Toward Work*: Not wanting to be like their workaholic Baby Boomer parents, Generation X makes a conscious effort to maintain a healthy work-life balance. This enables them to be involved in numerous activities outside of the office.

2. *What is Important*: Generation X is not afraid to work long hours or put forth extraordinary effort. They are willing to do whatever

is necessary to get the job done. However, they are not interested in spending excess time in the office if they don't have to. They want to come in, complete their work, and go home.

3. *Rewarding Quality Performance*: Generation X is interested in receiving formal acknowledgement for a job well done in a variety of ways. This includes pay increases, promotions, and high-impact projects that will lead to new opportunities. Additionally, less traditional perks are also valued (i.e., flex time, working from home, etc.).

4. *Leadership*: Generation X will put forth exceptional effort for leaders who have integrity and are willing to go the extra mile for them. Though they traditionally respect authority figures, Generation X is only willing to put forth maximum effort for leaders who consistently have their words and actions align, and who lead by example. If leaders continually fail to follow through, members of Generation X will quickly lose respect for them.

5. *Teamwork and Collaboration*: Generation X is comfortable working alone or in a team environment. As the first generation to come from a dual income family, Generation X has been self-managing since they were young, so most feel comfortable on their own. However, as youths who spent many days and nights as latchkey children, in Boys & Girls Clubs, and in after school programs, this generation has also been involved in teambuilding and knows exactly what it takes to successfully collaborate with others.

6. *Sharing Information*: Generation X believes transparency in the workplace is beneficial. This is especially true when it comes to sharing information. They believe knowledge is power and the more information is shared, the stronger an organization can become.

7. *Communication Medium*: Generation X prefers a blend of face-to-face communication and high-tech alternatives (i.e., email, IM, text, WebEx, etc.). Preference is usually based on the medium that is easiest to use for that specific situation.

8. *Innovation*: As the conduit between Baby Boomers and Millennials, Generation X balances interest in change with skepticism. They approach each innovation with tentative optimism, while weighing the pros and cons. They are interested in improving the workplace, but do not want to change something just for the sake of change.

9. *Technology*: Though not afraid of technological advances, members of Generation X are not typically early adopters. Instead, they appreciate the opportunity to observe how the new technology works before investing in it.

10. *Commitment to the Company*: Though Generation X will commit to their current role, they are criticized for not having a deep attachment to a particular employer. This is primarily because of the ease at which they move from company to company. This makes it important to keep them engaged in the activities that they are involved in and make sure they have the opportunity to progress. Though not willing to take any job for career advancement, they are willing to change companies for the right position.

11. *Dress/Attire*: Generation X doesn't see the need to consistently wear formal clothes to work. While they are willing to dress up for important meetings and client visits, they do not feel it is necessary to be more formal than business casual on a typical workday.

12. *Intangibles*: Generation X brought corporate social responsibility into the limelight and reinforced the importance of philanthropy and investing in the community. They believe wholeheartedly in giving back. Additionally, they prefer workplaces with diversity, informality, and fun.

BABY BOOMERS—BORN 1946 TO 1964

1. *Mentality Toward Work*: Baby Boomers live to work and often associate who they are with what they do. Work has always been an anchor in their lives and they are proud of how many hours they put in at the office. Though they could be classified as workaholics, they believe everyone should spend long hours in the workplace to be productive and demonstrate commitment.

2. *What is Important*: Baby Boomers are process-focused and often value following well-defined procedures over getting results. Though they want to be productive, their interest heavily favors developing and following a course of action to complete their

responsibilities. Additionally, time in the office is as important as producing results.

3. *Rewarding Quality Performance*: Baby Boomers want to be compensated financially for a job well done. They believe money is the ultimate way to reward employees.

4. *Leadership*: Leadership is held in high regard by Baby Boomers. While some authority figures have to earn their respect, most Baby Boomers are inclined to respect those in leadership positions. However, similar to believing time in the office is as important as productivity, many Baby Boomers feel that they have waited in line for their predecessors to pass the torch and it is now their turn to lead. This can create friction if Baby Boomers are passed over and the situation is exponentially more volatile if they are overlooked for someone considerably younger.

5. *Teamwork and Collaboration*: Though not always opposed to working on a team, there isn't an intrinsic desire to collaborate with others. Baby Boomers believe junior roles and younger generations should defer to employees who have been in the workplace for extended periods of time. They don't always understand the need for excessive games, "unnecessary" team building activities, or a collaborative environment in which everyone can participate.

6. *Sharing Information*: Sharing information is strictly on a need-to-know basis. Based on the lack of strong interest to collaborate with others and minimal desire to innovate, sharing information and including people is not a primary objective. While Baby Boomers are not opposed to sharing information with colleagues when they are working on a project together, they are only willing to include people if there is a need.

7. *Communication Medium*: Baby Boomers prefer face-to-face communication (or telephone) to other forms of correspondence such as email, IM, text, WebEx, etc. They will go to great lengths to gather together for a meeting rather than use technological resources. Though often less convenient than other forms of communication, they prefer in-person dialogue. This aligns very closely with their belief that people need to be in the office to be productive.

8. *Innovation*: Immersed in tradition and comfortable with their surroundings, Baby Boomers are not typically interested in

innovation. Though they will support innovation if they can see how it will benefit the company, they do not understand the need to continually modify operations, develop new processes, or incorporate new technology.

9. *Technology*: Closely aligned with innovation, technological advances are not a high priority for many Baby Boomers. Having not grown up in a technologically rich environment, using (and understanding) new technology is difficult. This problem is made worse due to the speed at which technological advances occur in today's world.

10. *Commitment to the Company*: Baby Boomers are exceptionally loyal to their company and will sacrifice their personal life for the benefit of the organization. Though they are open to new opportunities at different organizations, many are at the tail end of their career, so would rather coast into retirement with their current company than uproot their routine to change jobs.

11. *Dress/Attire*: Much like their parents' generation (who dressed up to get on an airplane), Baby Boomers believe it is important to look professional for certain activities, including work. Though not as conservative as their parents, Baby Boomers do prefer more formal attire at the office.

12. *Intangibles*: Baby Boomers have a strong work ethic and a great deal of appreciation for tradition. While these are great attributes, they can lead to being rigid and not knowing how to adapt to changes. This is evident in many Baby Boomers' appreciation for the book, *Who Moved My Cheese?* The book addresses managing change in the workplace and adapting to situations that are unfamiliar. Though the Generation X and Millennial crowd thought the message was relatively simplistic, Baby Boomers lauded it, claiming that they couldn't understand how to manage change before reading this book.[1]

IDEOLOGIES AND PREFERENCES

TABLE 2.1

Ideologies and Preferences

	Millennials	Generation X	Baby Boomers
Mentality toward work	Work to live	Work-life balance	Live to work
What is important	Productivity and results; when and where they do the work doesn't matter	Results-focused; want to come in, do their job, then go home	Process focused; time in the office is equally important to producing results
Rewarding quality performance	Intangible benefits; time off, working from home, high profile projects	Blend between traditional and nontraditional rewards	Financial
Leadership	Most respect leadership, but some feel that leaders are out of touch	Respects leaders who lead by example	Respects leadership; believes it is their turn to lead because they've paid their dues
Teamwork and collaboration	Prefer to work in a team environment	Comfortable working in a team or independently	Prefer to work independently or where there is a hierarchy; doesn't always see the value of teams
Sharing information	Fear of missing out (FOMO)	Knowledge is power; sharing information is beneficial	Only shares if there is a need to know
Communication medium	Technology: email, IM, text, WebEx, etc.	Whatever medium is easiest	Face-to-face, phone
Innovation	Change is good; out with the old, in with the new	Skeptical, though will try it if it adds value	Resistant to innovation and change
Technology	Early adopters	Skeptical, though will try it if it adds value	Slow to adopt new technology
Commitment to the company	Minimal; will change jobs if an intriguing opportunity is available	Moves easily between jobs; no long-term commitment	Long-term commitment; very loyal to the company and people they work with
Dress/attire	Business casual/casual	Business casual	Formal/business casual
Intangibles	Social media, multi-tasking, technology, philanthropy, diversity, friendly, corporate social responsibility	Corporate social responsibility, philanthropy, informal, fun, diversity	Tradition, work ethic, commitment, rigid, struggle to adapt to change

BRINGING IT ALL TOGETHER

Employees from all walks of life and every corner of the globe are thrust together in today's economy. No longer are organizations separated by culture, ethnicity, race, or sex. Instead, they maintain a dynamically rich blend of diverse talent that works side-by-side. This is true for employees of various ages as well. While in the past, employees would typically be surrounded by colleagues who were in the same generation, this is no longer the case. Millennials, Generation X, and Baby Boomers now work hand-in-hand with one another more than ever.

This can be challenging because of the unique ideologies and preferences that each generation has and the inherent mentality that they all often possess; their way is the best way and members of other age groups simply don't get it. This common, albeit self-focused attitude is what can create challenges in the workplace. Take inventory of each generation's ideologies and preferences, recognize commonalities and differences, and discover how to enable employees from every generation to perform optimally.

ENDNOTE

1 S. Johnson and K. Blanchard, *Who Moved My Cheese?* (New York: G.P. Putnam's Sons, 1998), pp. 3–10.

3

The 12 Types of Millennials in the Workplace

While defining the customary ideologies and preferences for each generation is helpful, it doesn't get to the core of the true strengths and weaknesses each employee possesses, nor does it unveil how to get the best out of the members on your team. Employee groups have different types of employees in the workplace that display a variety of characteristics. While there are overarching commonalities that employees in each generation possess, employees have unique attributes that they bring to the workplace every day that helps to distinguish who they are and how they work.

This is especially true for Millennials. While Millennial employees traditionally possess common beliefs and shared perspectives with the 12 workplace topics discussed in the previous chapter, they are employees with diverse skillsets, assorted abilities, and wide-ranging interests. They can't be lumped into one large group that doesn't allow for individuality or uniqueness. Millennial employees vary as much as any other generation, with behavioral traits and mentalities toward work covering the entire spectrum, from passionate and motivated to unfocused and apathetic. Because of this, throwing all Millennials together and typecasting them as one would cause more harm than good.

However, there are types of Millennial employees that have specific tendencies within this generation that are consistent. These Millennial archetypes have characteristics that help to define their unique talents and abilities and approach toward work. So, while general ideologies and preferences offer a broad view of this generation's employees, the archetypes deliver a more in-depth analysis and provide context for why certain stereotypes often materialize.

While no two employees are the same and no Millennial fits into one archetype exclusively, the description of each archetype provides a more profound understanding of the behavioral traits many Millennials possess. This enables leaders to have a broader knowledge base of the types of Millennials in the workforce.

Following are the 12 archetypes that describe Millennials currently in the workplace. These archetypes represent both positive and negative traits that Millennials possess and help to eliminate the idea that all in this generation are the same. More than just descriptions and broad strokes that define stereotypical behavior, strengths and weaknesses are shared for each archetype. Additionally, the descriptions cover the actions these archetypes take when they are at their worst and reveal how to tap into their unique skills to get the best out of them. This ensures managers will be able to maximize each Millennial's potential.

THE SELF-CENTERED CELEBRITY

The "Self-Centered Celebrity" is your stereotypical Millennial if there ever was one; smart, well-educated, and beautiful, she has been given every opportunity to succeed. Though not averse to hard work, the classic daddy's little girl has always had the best of everything growing up and could be viewed as entitled. However, she is able to deliver considerable value to the organization. The Self-Centered Celebrity is a powerful influencer in her circle and has the ability to encourage colleagues to act in a certain way, follow a trend, or start a movement. But, she doesn't get along with everyone and is often the leader of a clique, and if you rub her the wrong way it is very difficult to get back on her good side. She can also be resentful and jealous, especially of those whom she doesn't get along with or whom she sees as competition. As the center of attention from a young age, it doesn't sit well with the Self-Centered Celebrity if someone else receives accolades for his or her work (even if he or she deserves it).

> *Strengths*: Powerful influencer, always on the cutting edge of style and technology, natural leader, knows how to get things done, excellent at collaborating, good at networking.

Weaknesses: Noncommittal, manipulative, involved in cliques, can make people feel unwanted, holds grudges, wants to get her way or else won't put forth considerable effort.

When she is at her worst: Accustomed to being the center of attention, this Millennial can become painfully unpleasant to work with if she is not included or doesn't get her way. Growing up, all she needed to do was ask for something and she got it. This entitled mentality can leave her believing that this should continue. She "deserves" to have the best of everything. While she can be an excellent employee capable of uniting a team and leading change, she can also be cliquey and willing to exclude people she doesn't get along with. This narcissistic approach makes it very hard for colleagues to work with her if they are on the outside looking in. Additionally, whatever you do, do not isolate the Self-Centered Celebrity. Her productivity will plummet and she will look for ways to leave the company.

How to bring out her best: Give the Self-Centered Celebrity high-visibility projects that require everyone in the company to get onboard. As a powerful influencer, she is able to motivate others and produce results, thus can be an important catalyst. Fuel her with opportunities to leverage her unique ability to unite people and create transformational change. Additionally, provide the Self-Centered Celebrity the opportunity to network and build connections for your department and organization. The Self-Centered Celebrity is great at developing relationships and forming alliances. By helping her use this talent, she will lay the groundwork for your department to have strong, long-term relationships for years to come.

THE STEADY DELIVERER

Regardless of the situation, project, or issue, you can count on the "Steady Deliverer." He is smart, hardworking, and always puts forth his best effort. He also has a zest for asking the right questions, challenging the status quo, and doing whatever he can to help the company. The Steady Deliverer is your model employee. He will take care of his responsibilities, always delivers results, and often takes on tasks that extend beyond his job description. With a unique ability to discover innovative solutions, the Steady Deliverer is consistently brought on to solve complex challenges. He cares about the company, his team, and the colleagues he works alongside, and will do whatever he can to help the business succeed. However, he can get overwhelmed with work, resulting in a reduction in performance, and doesn't always speak up when there are conflicting priorities.

Strengths: Hard worker, dedicated, willing to go above and beyond, focused, possesses institutional knowledge, savvy, problem solver, positive attitude.

Weaknesses: Can't say no, frustrated with heavy workload, doesn't communicate when overwhelmed/overworked, could get worn out.

When he is at his worst: The Steady Deliverer is at his worst when he is given numerous projects at the same time. As the go-to employee, he is always being given tasks that are outside of his traditional responsibilities. Not wanting to ever let anyone down, he instinctively takes these projects on without blinking. Though willing to take on anything sent his way, he secretly gets frustrated with the workload. Late nights in the office and midnight emails deplete him of energy and increase the risk of him leaving the job for something that is less cumbersome.

How to bring out his best: Recognize the accomplishments of the Steady Deliverer whenever he goes above and beyond. As a prominent employee who always delivers results, keeping him engaged and motivated is critical. This is more challenging than it would seem. Everyone loads work onto the Steady Deliverer, so he is constantly at risk of becoming overwhelmed. Shield him from unnecessary work that could be given to others and eliminate (or at least reduce) the number of times he is burning the midnight oil. Also, prone to completing work that is above his pay grade, ensure he doesn't do his supervisor's job. Instead, elevate his status and give him the promotion he deserves. He is a quality employee that you can't afford to lose.

THE KNOW-IT-ALL

This Millennial is a genius, in his eyes. Loud, abrasive, and possessing a unique zest for inserting himself into every situation that will allow him to feel superior, the "Know-It-All" incessantly tries to find ways to make himself look powerful and intelligent. This is most evident during conversations that have him talking down to many of his colleagues (and in some cases his superiors) in an attempt to elevate himself. The Know-It-All loves to condescendingly "mansplain" everything he can, passing along his wisdom to anyone who will take the time to listen. Unfortunately, in almost every situation his need to provide accurate (or relevant) information during conversations is trumped by his overwhelming desire to get the last word. This disdainful approach toward communication makes it unnecessary to speak the truth. Instead, his goals are to prove he is intelligent, win the argument, or be seen as important.

Strengths: Confidence, take-charge attitude, wants to be involved in everything.

Weaknesses: Arrogant, possesses more confidence than ability, insecure, taker, only sees what others can do for him, lacks social grace, minimal compassion, narcissist, bully, wears on people, most relationships are one-sided and end poorly.

When he is at his worst: Whenever high-powered leaders are present, the Know-It-All feels the need to impress them. He wants recognition and approval from leadership, so will do whatever is necessary to make himself look important, even if that means tearing down colleagues. The Know-It-All also struggles mightily when a topic is being discussed that is outside of his knowledge base. As an employee who will do anything to be the center of attention, he will try either to change the subject or add anecdotal information that lacks substance—anything to have the focus shift back in his direction.

How to bring out his best: Not good at building long-term relationships, this "expert" wants immediate gratification and is interested in being seen as a shining star in the organization. This makes him a results-oriented employee who is focused on producing. Take advantage of this by including him in short-term projects with tight deadlines that are extremely detail-oriented. As a task-focused individual who doesn't often build strong relationships, the Know-It-All typically places more emphasis on producing results over developing long-term friendships. He will go to great lengths to deliver value at any cost, including fracturing relationships to get the job done. Additionally, because he is prone to frustrating others, working with him can be exhausting. Short-term projects enable the Know-It-All to execute his responsibilities, and then move on before he pushes people over the edge. To ensure he remains engaged in every project, provide him positive reinforcement and validation so that he knows you appreciate his work and the value he delivers.

THE HIGH PERFORMER

This Millennial is brilliant, hardworking, and dedicated. Quite simply, she is everything you could ever want from an employee, and if you merely saw her resume on paper, you would do anything to have her on your team! Everyone wants the "High Performer," because everyone knows that if you have her, you win! She is a superstar who possesses the unique analytical and quantitative skills that enable her to thrive in any environment. This allows you to put her in various roles in the organization, knowing that she will find a way to bring out the best in herself and others. The only problem with this Millennial is that there aren't more like her. She is a rare breed of employee, less than 1% of Millennials possess these unique characteristics.

Strengths: Smart, hardworking, dedicated, well-educated, socially aware, able to work with both senior leaders and frontline employees, analytical, driven, committed to the organization.

Weaknesses: Gets bored if not challenged, well-known in the industry and could get poached by a recruiter.

When she is at her worst: When the High Performer is at her worst, *you* are the problem. This Millennial is wildly talented and has skills that far exceed almost everyone else in the company. If you are overbearing and try to hold onto this employee too tightly, her productivity will plummet. The High Performer also struggles when she is given work that doesn't challenge her. Basic tasks that do not push her to use her skills or fail to deliver any considerable value leave her uninspired and lacking the desire to put forth a concerted effort. She wants to be continually challenged and could get frustrated if she is not contributing the way she knows she can. Do not lump the High Performer in with every other Millennial. Treat her with distinct value. She is a future leader of your organization.

How to bring out her best: Just give her a project and get out of the way. Entering the workforce with a unique understanding of how to get things done, the High Performer produces extraordinary value. Provide her challenging work that requires analytical and quantitative analysis. This will enable her to tap into her diverse skill set while simultaneously growing. Additionally, provide the High Performer with the opportunity to lead high-visibility, high-value projects that provide access to C-level leadership. This Millennial doesn't want to waste her time on activities that do not serve a valuable purpose or enable her to grow. She knows her value and the type of skills she possesses. Empower her to consistently use her talents.

THE SOCIAL MEDIA QUEEN

The "Social Media Queen" loves to post everything online. Whether it is personal or professional, you don't have to wonder for too long what she is doing or how she is feeling, she is always updating her status on social media. While she can be a deep thinker, quite often simple gestures go a long way in helping to make the Social Media Queen's day better. Additionally, though she is willing to put in a hard day's work, she can lose track of time when she is surfing the web. This causes her productivity to drop.

Strengths: Great at collaboration, gets along with everyone, outgoing and inclusive, loves to support the organization and get involved.

Weaknesses: Doesn't know her own abilities, easily distracted, won't always stand up for herself, not focused.

When she is at her worst: More excited about social media than work, this Millennial's productivity has an immediate downward spiral when she is not actively engaged. Though not intending to be lazy, the Social Media Queen can easily become focused on her phone for hours at a time if she is not consistently provided enough work to do. This is primarily because she is more interested in updating her status and commenting on what is trending than following through with her responsibilities.

How to bring out her best: With the unique ability to start a movement, the Social Media Queen is at her best when she can leverage her skill of collaborating with others. Her ability to connect with people, both virtually and in person, creates the opportunity for the company to make (potentially unpopular) changes seem positive when she is involved. Make sure she is part of any initiative or project that requires large-scale change. This will ensure the company culture does not waver in spite of changes being introduced. Additionally, quite often the Social Media Queen doesn't understand the transferrable skills social media presents (e.g., marketing, customer service, community management, etc.). Broaden the Social Media Queen's knowledge base. Show her how her skills can be used in a variety of ways in the business by setting her up to shadow colleagues who work in functional areas that could use her talents. This will enable the Social Media Queen to leverage her skills while growing her confidence.

THE TECHNOLOGY WIZ

The "Technology Wiz" has a unique skill set that is invaluable to the company. Whether it is creating reports to automate manual activities, working on a new technology that will simplify production, or teaching fellow colleagues how to use a new program, the Technology Wiz is always delivering value. Surprisingly, he doesn't always realize that his work is important or that he is appreciated; to him, it is just another day. This is partly because the Technology Wiz loves what he does. To him, doing this shouldn't be classified as work, he enjoys it too much! Further, not wanting to be the center of attention, the Technology Wiz is often quite content doing his job and making his boss look good. He doesn't want (or need) to be the focus. Playing with data, developing code, or working on a new platform is so much more fun than anything else! However, if you get him one-on-one, he is more than happy to share all of the exciting projects he is involved in.

Strengths: Humble, dedicated, loves the job, enjoys automating manual tasks, can fix anything, can quantify everything, has a wealth of knowledge and skills, very focused on producing results.

Weaknesses: Doesn't like attention, won't inform you if something is wrong unless you ask, skills don't often extend beyond IT, doesn't like public speaking.

When he is at his worst: The Technology Wiz is at his worst when he has a leader who provides guidance and direction that is neither rational nor helpful. This is primarily because it creates the inherent belief that the manager lacks basic understanding as to what the Technology Wiz actually does and how he brings value to the organization. The Technology Wiz also struggles when he is pulled from IT projects or given work that lacks the need for a certain technological prowess. When this occurs, he typically becomes uninterested in producing and starts questioning the motivation behind management decisions.

How to bring out his best: The Technology Wiz is energized by having the opportunity to work independently, so provide him autonomy every chance you get. This will enable him to use his intuitive nature to discover innovative ways to create value. More generally, while almost everyone sees how important this Millennial's work is, quite often the Technology Wiz lacks awareness. He doesn't see the value he is producing nor does he understand how truly important he is to the company. Make an effort to celebrate his accomplishments every chance you get. Though the Technology Wiz is often an introvert not wanting to be the center of attention, he does appreciate being recognized for a job well done. Finally, while he loves his work, monitor the number of hours this Millennial is putting in each week. Burnout with the Technology Wiz is a risk due to him taking his work home. Make sure he takes time for himself.

THE VICTIM

Everything is a fight with the "Victim." As if he has been shortchanged at every possible turn, this Millennial believes that the entire world is against him. Even situations that do not involve him directly suddenly become a huge priority, only to be short-lived until the next catastrophic atrocity occurs, and he diverts his attention to that. In essence, the sky is always falling. Instead of working hard to become successful, he instinctively sees the negative in every situation. It often becomes so bad that others receive his assignments to avoid the inevitable arguments with him. This creates even more of a tailspin for the Victim because he feels that he is not getting the opportunity to be involved or move up in the company. Though he will typically have at least one attractive skill that enabled him to land his current role, the value he provides pales in comparison to the endless effort it takes to get him to stop causing problems and stay focused on work.

Strengths: Has a unique set of skills, detail-oriented, willing to own projects that he is good at.

Weaknesses: Ready to fight at a moment's notice, never happy, noncommittal, poisonous to the company culture, clock-watcher, angry, not trusting of others, rigid and inflexible.

When he is at his worst: Sadly, the Victim is at his worst almost 95% of the time. He trusts almost no one and sees everyone as an enemy who is less intelligent and less talented than he is. The Victim complains about everything, is in constant crisis mode, and always believes he is being shortchanged somehow. Include him in something and he will tell you that you are doing it wrong, do not include him and he will blow up because you aren't letting him in. Because of this, most endings are no surprise: the Victim either abruptly quits or is fired.

How to bring out his best: Unfortunately, options are limited. Though you can curb the "victim mentality," it is often so entrenched in the Victim's entitled mindset and rooted in a lack of reality that there is nothing you can do. For those who can be salvaged, provide engaging projects that enable him to use his unique skills. Consistently show him what he needs to do to grow with the company. This will enable him to see what actions he needs to take to succeed.

THE GRINDER

This Millennial is the backbone of your organization and is willing to do whatever is necessary to make your company succeed! Far from being raised with a silver spoon in her mouth, the "Grinder" relentlessly pursues greatness while overcoming any obstacle that could possibly get in her way. With an unrelenting spirit that will not let her give up, the Grinder believes she is able to accomplish anything. This is because she has seen far more challenging circumstances in her personal life than anything the job could possibly throw at her. Further, her skill set within the organization is unmatched. She is a subject matter expert who knows how to get things done, and if she can't do it on her own, she will find someone who can help. Her relentless nature creates a need for her to excel at her job, so she works to master everything she can. However, while the Grinder is an excellent worker, there are times that she acts in ways that are less than refined. Though she will always maintain integrity, she can be a little rough around the edges.

Strengths: Dedicated, loyal, friendly, hardworking, willing to do whatever is necessary to help the company, team player, subject matter expert, extremely valuable to the organization.

Weaknesses: Doesn't always see the big picture, can be unsophisticated, doesn't understand her skill set or why she is so valuable to the company, not good at delegating.

When she is at her worst: This Millennial has unique skills that have enabled her to become successful. When she is unable to use the talents she has acquired and tools she has mastered, she loses interest. The reason she is so passionate is because she worked exceptionally hard to refine her abilities. Not providing her the opportunity to use them creates a downward spiral.

How to bring out her best: The Grinder has faced more obstacles in her personal and professional life than almost any of her counterparts (often without the support of others), and knows what it is like to walk through difficult challenges. Loyalty is beyond important to this employee. Give her even the slightest amount of support and she will go to war for you! She is also a self-starter, so give her a challenge and get out of the way, she will find a solution! She beams with pride when she is able to solve a complex problem. Provide continual encouragement to the Grinder. This will inspire her to continue working hard while simultaneously strengthening the bond you two have together.

THE I'M TOO GOOD FOR THAT

Much like the Victim, the "I'm too Good for That" Millennial is painfully difficult to work with. His work ethic is subpar, he lacks basic knowledge of certain areas in his job, and he is unwilling to perform activities that he deems are beneath him. Nevertheless, he still believes he excels at everything he does. Though there are colleagues who fulfill the exact same role as him, complete all of the tasks that they are assigned, and produce better results, the I'm too Good for That foolishly believes that he is *the guy* on the team who everyone looks up to. Caught up in his own little world, he always has some piece of wisdom to pass along about how others can do more and be better, failing to understand that his work ethic, abilities, and knowledge have serious holes in them. He is also always bragging about how he could make twice as much money with companies on the other side of town, and how his dynamic skills would finally be put to good use if he changed organizations. In reality, he is all talk. Anyone who has basic knowledge of the company sees right through this façade.

Strengths: Good at certain parts of the job, self-assured, doesn't get sucked into interoffice politics.

Weaknesses: Overconfident, arrogant, complacent, narcissist, not attune to reality, lacks social awareness, not respected by colleagues, noncommittal, not a good team player.

When he is at his worst: When surrounded by people who buy into his B.S., the I'm too Good for That becomes intolerable. His massive ego grows as people fill his need for attention. As an employee who actively endorses himself every chance he gets, the I'm too Good for That feeds off people who will listen to him talk about how he is exceedingly talented. This problem intensifies the longer this Millennial is stuck in the same position. To overcompensate for his lack of career growth, he continually expresses how valuable he is while simultaneously taking on less and less. This inevitably leads to the continued inflation of his ego, "supreme" abilities, and lack of productivity.

How to bring out his best: With expertise in certain areas of the job, provide the I'm too Good for That with tasks that align with these skills. This will ensure he is able to use his talents to the fullest extent. However, do not let him rest on his laurels. Highlight areas that he is not proficient in and challenge him to improve. Push him to expand his skill set and grow. With a large ego, this can be exceptionally powerful due to the instinctive desire of the I'm too Good for That to be seen by colleagues as an expert in his craft. He wants to be the "go-to" employee who has all the answers.

THE RELIABLE BUDDY

The "Reliable Buddy" is great to be around. Easygoing, energetic, and always in a good mood, the Reliable Buddy seems to brighten everyone's day the moment they cross paths with him. He works hard, is always willing to lend a helping hand, and will go the extra mile for you, if you should ever need it. He is your classic "glass half full" employee and can always see the good in every situation. However, he doesn't have the best skills and lacks potential for upward mobility. But that doesn't matter to him: he enjoys what he does and where he works, so he is quite content in his current environment.

> *Strengths*: Positive energy, encouraging, culture carrier, hard worker, loyal to the company and the people he works with, friendly.
>
> *Weaknesses*: Skills are limited, lacks sincere interest in career growth, doesn't see the big picture, won't acknowledge bad news or big challenges directly.
>
> *When he is at his worst*: The Reliable Buddy is at his worst when he is given a task that he has never done before. As an employee with limited skills and minimal confidence, he doesn't have the ability to discover creative solutions to difficult problems. This issue is often magnified by his unwillingness to accept that a problem exists in the first place. The Reliable Buddy doesn't like to acknowledge bad news, so has a tendency to pretend nothing is wrong. This can cause bigger problems if issues spiral out of control.
>
> *How to bring out his best*: Provide the Reliable Buddy work that he knows how to do and is comfortable completing. As a dependable employee, he won't let you down. After he has mastered basic tasks, give him small, bite-sized duties that gently stretch him. This will instill confidence in the Reliable Buddy while enabling him to grow. Additionally, bring him into meetings where difficult problems are discussed. By enabling him to see how challenges are worked through, he will become more interested in solving problems instead of not acknowledging that they exist.

THE APATHETIC UNDERACHIEVER

This Millennial is shy and unassuming. Though gifted in many ways, she is quite content staying in her comfort zone, fulfilling her responsibilities, and going about her day without pushing too hard. While the "Apathetic Underachiever" does a good job, she just isn't sure if her actions are exactly what the boss is looking for. She lacks confidence and needs reassurance that she is doing what is expected. Her skills could enable her to be so much more, if only she cared or had someone push her. Her willingness to be content with where she is currently exemplifies the telltale sign that she doesn't have the motivation to pursue anything greater. The Apathetic Underachiever is happy with mediocrity and couldn't care less if she worked for your company or somewhere else. Finally, though she is capable of moving up in the organization, she lacks the initiative to take on a leadership role, gladly passing that perceived burden onto someone else.

Strengths: Talented, smart, unique skill set, has potential, willing to do whatever is asked, doesn't seek the limelight.

Weaknesses: Not confident, won't speak up, content with fading into the background, doesn't push herself, needs encouragement to produce, doesn't care.

When she is at her worst: This Millennial is at her worst when she has nothing to do and no one is challenging her. This provides the Apathetic Underachiever time to shop online, sneak out to Starbucks, and text with friends. As a typical 9–5 employee, this suits her just fine. Her inclination has always been to watch the clock instead of focus on being productive.

How to bring out her best: Constant communication with this Millennial is imperative for her to stay on task. Though the Apathetic Underachiever possesses considerable talent, she either doesn't have the confidence to believe that she is doing her job correctly or gets distracted by things that are unrelated to her work (i.e., social media, texting with friends, etc.). Regardless of the reason, she needs to be reassured that her actions are mapping to what the boss wants. Provide consistent validation and support. Though it may seem like a burden initially, it will pay dividends in the long run. Continual encouragement will spark her motivation and increase her confidence, enabling her to be more productive.

THE FRUSTRATED PRODUCER

The "Frustrated Producer" is a great employee who is loyal, dedicated, and willing to go above and beyond; her only problem, she doesn't like other Millennials. The Frustrated Producer is often someone born right after the switch from Generation X to Millennial occurred. While there is no question she falls into the age range of a Millennial, the Frustrated Producer does her best to distance herself from her generation due to the negative connotations that are often associated with this group. Though she is committed to the job and her colleagues, the Frustrated Producer becomes infuriated when Millennials display carelessness toward their work or others. She doesn't understand how certain people are able to possess such a lack of concern for everything around them. In essence, she loathes the stereotypical Millennial and everything they stand for.

Strengths: Hard worker, dedicated, committed to the job, friendly, willing to go above and beyond for colleagues.

Weaknesses: Can be impatient (especially toward other Millennials), negative attitude toward other Millennials, doesn't acknowledge that she possesses any stereotypical Millennial characteristics.

When she is at her worst: For some reason, the Frustrated Producer has an innate disgust for "typical" Millennial behavior. So, when she experiences Millennials acting in accordance with what is deemed inappropriate, she becomes incensed. This leads to a lack of productivity on her end because she is consumed with frustrations toward fellow members of her generation. This often makes it difficult for her to work with other Millennials because they drive the Frustrated Producer crazy!

How to bring out her best: The Frustrated Producer works best when she is surrounded by other high-functioning employees. She is used to working hard and delivering results, so when she is paired with employees who lack discipline, she becomes irritated. By connecting the Frustrated Producer with employees who are also results-driven, she will remain focused on fulfilling her responsibilities instead of being frustrated with colleagues.

BRINGING IT ALL TOGETHER

As shared earlier, no Millennial falls into a single archetype. Though there will inevitably be certain defining characteristics that stand out for each Millennial in the workplace, no one fits into a single category. Employees are inevitably a blend of the 12 archetypes discussed.

Don't take everyone at face value. While many people are set in their ways, employees do change based on circumstances, especially when you place emphasis on bringing out their best. Though certain behaviors can certainly be frustrating, many characteristics can be modified (and improved) if addressed appropriately. Dig deep to find the unique attributes that you can leverage to enhance the productivity of each Millennial in your organization. Take an active role in pulling out their strengths.

Section II

Everything Has Changed

For over 50 years, Toys "R" Us was *the* place to shop for toys. The exhilarating experience of walking into the enormous store that had rows and rows of toys was every child's dream. The latest dolls, coolest action figures, best games, and newest electronics made it wildly exciting to enter the huge building, purchase a toy, and rush home to play with it. What could be more fun?

Toys "R" Us rode this wildly successful strategy for the better part of a century. However, as the dawn of the internet came and went, they didn't innovate. They took their success for granted and maintained the "business is good enough" mentality that ultimately led to them declaring bankruptcy in 2017, with plans to close all of its US-based stores in 2018.

Toys "R" Us made two fatal errors. The first error involved outsourcing delivery of internet sales. Instead of leveraging the use of the internet and capitalizing on being the market leader in toys, Toys "R" Us outsourced the delivery of internet purchases to Amazon. This enabled customers to embrace buying toys from a retailer other than Toys "R" Us.

The second error involved remaining stagnant with their business model and how they set up their stores. In the second half of the twentieth century, customers were comfortable just getting a toy; they didn't need a unique experience to remember. This has changed. Many of those who are not buying on the internet now crave an interactive experience that captures their interest.

Challengers in the market noticed this and altered their business model to meet this demand and gain competitive advantage. This is evident from the doll store, American Girl. Contrary to Toys "R" Us, American Girl offers more than just a doll for young girls to take home. The company delivers magical experiences that are not soon forgotten. The opportunity for young children to meander throughout the elegant store, have teatime with their doll, and pop in for a visit to the hair salon, makes a visit to the American Girl store a special occasion that can be cherished.

Alternatively, even if the end goal is to merely purchase a doll and bring it back to your child, going to Toys "R" Us is still not the best choice. A customer could easily buy a doll at Walmart while shopping for groceries or jump online and have it delivered to them by Amazon in less than 24 hours. Both options are more efficient and cheaper.

In the end it is simple. Toys "R" Us failed because it didn't change to meet the needs of the market. Instead, it chose to keep business as it had always been: rows of toys stacked from floor to ceiling—an outdated method of selling merchandise. The company could have built giant playgrounds, set up a race track for kids to test remote-control cars, or put in a coffeehouse for parents to relax while their children played with dolls or action figures: anything to create a stir and keep up with market demand.

Instead, they did nothing, remained complacent, and ultimately suffered a slow and tragic collapse. In a time of exceptional competition and rapid transformation, their unwillingness to adapt led to their demise.[1]

****

As the onetime leader in toys, no one could have ever imagined that Toys "R" Us would die. The powerhouse that consistently led the way in the industry has reached the end of the road. This is the unmistakable reality for every industry, market, and company. Nothing remains the same. Business is always changing, and you are at risk if you are unwilling or unable to adapt.

Changing with the times is important to meet business needs and is equally important to meet changing employee needs. The uniqueness of employees, both young and old, requires distinct management. Though it may seem crazy to change management techniques and operational activities for businesses that have been successful for many years, the importance of reflecting on both human performance and business operations is critical.

Workplaces are constantly evolving as people, products, and industries go through seasons of change. Not surprisingly, this makes those who rest on the laurels of yesteryear vulnerable. Employees now crave new experiences, different environments, and unique opportunities. This is especially true for Millennials. Because of this, companies that willingly sacrifice taking action for maintaining the status quo inevitably become vulnerable to Millennials departing for greener pastures.

ENDNOTE

[1] G. Vaynerchuk, Innovate or die, online video, YouTube, last modified October 3, 2017, https://www.youtube.com/watch?v=WdYtoj4KSeU.

4

It's NOT about the Money!!!

Money is the only thing that matters! If you want to increase productivity and improve retention, all you need to do is increase an employee's wage. It is that simple.

This is a common mentality for a lot of leaders, especially those who fall outside of the Millennial generation. However, the notion that job satisfaction and a strong work ethic are completely dependent on financial compensation is inaccurate and outdated.

While compensation is a motivator that can generate specific behavior within an organization, research shows that in today's economy money is only a driver for engagement when it will provide a lifestyle change. Incremental increases in pay will not provide a deeper level of engagement, they will only generate short-term compliance. In short, money doesn't solve problems. It is only a short-term fix to a long-term issue.

This is especially true for Millennials! Members of this generation are not captivated by small bumps in salary or trivial increases in their hourly wage. They want a workplace that energizes them and speaks to their inner soul. This is lost on most leaders. They can't appreciate this way of thinking or disparate rationale. In the past, money was the ultimate motivator and served as *the* driver for improving performance. In essence, if you wanted employees to perform a certain way, you needed to increase their wages, and theoretically, the bigger the pay increase, the better the results.[1]

Employees from previous generations, especially Baby Boomers, were very focused on increasing their wages and were drawn to improving their financial stability whenever they had the opportunity. As young adults, they pinched pennies every chance they had and were loyal to their bank account at any cost. Having a stable financial future by saving money and moving up the corporate ladder was the quintessential focus.

For these members of the workforce, this mentality has not changed. Many of them still maintain this perspective and believe that their subordinates want the same thing. Extrinsic motivators were the reason they worked so hard and provided them the opportunity to get to where they are today. Deep down, they believe that everyone has a similar mindset. A good wage and career advancement are the prototypical motivators for every employee.

Though an increase in salary does often encourage a change in behavior, it is usually a short-term adjustment to appease leadership. This approach aligns closely to the way a donkey chases after a carrot on a stick; once the animal gets the coveted vegetable, its behavior reverts back to the way it acted previously.

This lacks sustainable results, especially for Millennials. Millennials' behaviors, customs, and overall way of life are different from members of previous generations (when they were the same age). Many Millennials willingly trade owning cars for taking Uber and Lyft, sleep in Airbnbs instead of staying at hotels, and postpone marriage and kids for travel and increased discretionary funds. And not surprisingly, just as their lifestyle is different from previous generations, so too is the way they approach their careers. Money and career advancement, while important, are not the driving forces that they once were. While increasing compensation for a job well done is appreciated and career advancement is valued, these incentives are gladly traded in for job satisfaction and personal fulfillment.

In short, it is not about the money! While that may have been a major motivator for members of previous generations, this is no longer the case. Millennials are not captivated by external rewards. Intrinsic motivators and intangible benefits are what truly inspire Millennials to perform.

Though no Millennial will typically turn down an increase in pay, opportunity for career advancement, or fringe benefits, these motivators do not carry as much weight as they used to. Millennials want to serve a valuable purpose, be empowered to deliver results, and work in a fulfilling environment. They are interested in unique experiences, spending time on activities that are important to them, and dependable leaders who they can rely on. Though this may seem idealistic to some and immaterial by others, Millennials are enthralled by these intrinsic motivators and intangible benefits. This is what pushes them to produce results.

THE THREE DRIVERS OF ENGAGEMENT

In essence, there are three overarching drivers of engagement: serving a valuable purpose, being empowered to deliver results, and working in a fulfilling environment. These drivers provide a foundation for critical ingredients that go into bringing out the best in Millennials and creating a workforce that is dedicated to organizational success over personal achievement. By leveraging these three drivers, organizations have a platform in which they can capitalize on the exceptional talents that Millennials bring to the workplace.

Serving a valuable purpose naturally engages because of the innate interest in being part of something that is greater than oneself. Instead of working hard to pursue something that solely focuses on themselves (i.e., a paycheck), Millennials are energized by having their actions extend beyond personal benefit. They enjoy working for the greater good. This transforms their mentality toward work due to the awareness that the benefit they are providing to the company can only be sustained if they continue fulfilling their responsibilities. Not surprisingly, like most employees, when Millennials are able to see how their contributions make a difference at the company or in the lives of others, they are interested in continuing to add this value, which ultimately leads to a stronger desire to achieve.

Being empowered to deliver results instills a sense of motivation that elevates performance while liberating people to pursue the most efficient way of fulfilling their role. When Millennials are empowered, they come to realize that they are not at the mercy of their supervisors to complete specific tasks a particular way. Instead, they are able to use their unique talents to find the best way to do their job. This ownership infuses them with excitement and is often a cornerstone for transforming potential into productivity.

Finally, working in a fulfilling environment enables Millennials to concentrate on their responsibilities and be engaged in their work instead of having to address issues that take away from primary objectives. More than just a facility to begrudgingly go to every day, Millennials want a workplace that brings them positive energy, fosters inspiration, and creates a quality setting in which they can put forth their best effort to utilize their unique skills. Millennials love fulfilling work environments because they offer a dynamic place in which they can embrace their responsibilities and be engaged in the tasks that they are assigned. They will gladly give up additional money for a strong workplace culture, work-life balance, having access to the right resources to complete their responsibilities, and the opportunity to improve their skills and grow with the company.[2]

TIME

Another considerable motivator for Millennials revolves around time. More than any other generation, Millennials have an insatiable desire to cram as much into their social lives as humanly possible. This is most apparent in the way they incessantly multitask. Though everyone has always juggled numerous activities in their lives, Millennials take it to the next level. Whether it is playing on their phone, combining multiple activities on a single night, or tying numerous errands together, Millennials are obsessed with time.

This holds true in the workplace as well. As brazen members of the workforce who have a never-ending desire to optimize their lives, how they spend their day is never far from their thoughts. This has Millennials believing that they should be able to structure their day however they see fit, instead of needing to conform to a traditional work schedule. This aligns closely with their aversion to being at the office until late at night.

Though many are willing to work 60+ hour workweeks, it isn't the way generations of yesteryear are used to. Laptops make Millennials mobile, so staying at the office until the sun goes down isn't necessary. Instead, Millennials are much more interested in working long hours in the comfort of their own home. Though not possible in every industry or function, the opportunity to work remotely to simplify work and life is extremely attractive.

Structuring their day to fit their schedule is exponentially more important when there are conflicts involving personal engagements. For example, Millennials will gladly work well into the night if they are provided the opportunity to sneak away from the office to take a two-hour lunch, play in an afternoon softball game, or grab dinner with friends. The freedom to balance their personal and professional lives enables them to immerse themselves in both without feeling as though they are missing anything.

Beyond just appreciating the opportunity to modify their schedule to meet their needs, Millennials are also fixated on results over merely putting in time at the office. They do not believe that employees who happen to be at work from 7 a.m. to 7 p.m. should be rewarded. Outcomes matter significantly more than just being present. As such, what does it matter if they answer a text in the middle of the day or listen to music in their cubicle, as long as they are getting their job done.

Some Millennials are so bold as to argue that people who are in the office longer but do not produce more should be admonished for their lack of efficiency. They believe employees who are able to fulfill their duties in less time should be valued for producing results quickly, rather than reprimanded for completing their responsibilities and departing.

Finally, Millennials can't stand when other people waste their time. Meetings that are unstructured or lack value and long-winded colleagues who seem to arbitrarily abuse the spotlight to belabor points push Millennials over the edge. Though most everyone gets frustrated when their time is wasted, Millennials are traditionally less forgiving. Living very active lives and prone to having numerous options available when their time could be potentially wasted (e.g., changing the television channel when there is a commercial, scrolling through social media while waiting in line, texting with friends while stopped at a red light, etc.), their options are limited while on the clock. Though most are not opposed to killing time while in the office, the notion that they will accept their time being wasted in less than ideal conditions or by someone else is inaccurate. Even while on the job, they value their time too much to waste it on activities that they are not invested in.

EXPERIENCE

When going out to eat, Millennials do not want to just enjoy a meal, they want a unique atmosphere; when posting on social media they can't just take a picture, they need to add a flashy filter and catchy hashtag; and when out on the town they are not interested in going to a generic bar, they require a captivating environment with festive drinks.

This is the same with their jobs. Millennials are not interested in merely walking in and punching a clock. They crave an experience. Millennials are fearless in the pursuit of what sets their soul on fire and will continue to search for a role they love until they find it! This means companies (and leaders) must challenge Millennials with interesting work. Regardless of the task, doing the same thing day after day with no variation lacks appeal for Millennials. They want unique opportunities that continually capture their interest and provide fresh energy. By fulfilling this craving, Millennials develop a connection to their job that stirs the desire to produce optimal results.

Though many in other generations had similar sentiments when they first started in their careers, an important distinction is the ease with which Millennials can change jobs. Unlike in the past, when people could only look through the want ads in the newspaper or attend a job fair when it was in town, employees can now look at prospective opportunities every day of the year via the Internet. This increases the risk of losing quality talent.

CONSISTENT DIRECTION

After a long flight home in a cramped seat on an airplane, almost everyone walks through the terminal with the same purpose—grab your luggage and get to your car so you can head home. Unfortunately, in these situations it is almost inevitable that you find yourself behind a group of well-meaning vacationers who seemingly have no idea how to navigate the airport. They walk fast, then slow down, stop to look for their ticket, then out of nowhere turn right into you. Already on edge, this experience can fill you with frustration. Navigating through the airport is easy when you know what to expect. The trouble is when people become unpredictable, it can drive you crazy.

This is the same feeling Millennials have when leaders fail to be consistent. Millennials can't stand when their company suddenly pivots in a new direction without notice or their manager continually wavers on a decision. Bouncing back and forth on managerial approaches, putting considerable effort in certain areas then quickly reverting to what was used in the past, and placing stock in "flavor of the month" ideas only to change direction again and again frustrates Millennials. They hate when their company abruptly changes directions for seemingly no reason or managers are half-pregnant with ideas, only to transform their approach quickly and unexpectedly.

While fluctuations are part of any business, requiring everyone to be flexible, unnecessary variations turn Millennials sour. Leaders (and companies) must remain committed to their approach. This is especially important when employing a new mindset that focuses less on external rewards and more on intrinsic motivators.

BRINGING IT ALL TOGETHER

Companies (and leaders) often fail to increase productivity and retention due to not changing their approach toward motivating employees. This causes them to miss out on the tangible benefits that could materialize if they used new ways to bring out their talents. More specifically, Millennials are different from employee groups of yesteryear, with money not being the predominant motivational interest. Companies must employ progressive leadership concepts that extend beyond a Millennial's pocketbook. By doing this, you will inspire the Millennial generation to produce exceptional results.

ENDNOTES

1 K. Phillips, *Employee LEAPS: Leveraging Engagement by Applying Positive Strategies* (New York: Business Expert Press, 2016), p. 11.
2 Ibid., pp. 9–23.

5

Transforming Operations to Meet the Needs of Today

In 1999, the movie *Office Space* came out in theaters brilliantly depicting the everyday work life of the "typical" employee who works in an office and hates his or her job. The movie's sympathetic portrayal of employees who despise their workplace is symbolic of "white-collar" personnel who begrudgingly show up uninspired and lacking desire to fulfill their responsibilities each and every day[1].

In the movie, everything about where the employees work is wrong. They serve no purpose, are not empowered to make a difference, and are not in a fulfilling environment. Though none of the employees in the film are Millennials, they all possess the same hatred toward their feeble employment that many in the workplace currently experience daily. While not every Millennial hates his or her job or despises the company he or she works for with the passion that the characters in the movie do, there is a unique connection that many Millennials have to the actors in the film: a paralyzing frustration with the way business is run and a lack of belief that things will ever get better.

Many Baby Boomers and Generation Xers tend to have limited sympathy for these Millennials. They had to suffer through the frustrating days that seemed to have no end and were able to survive, so why should it be any different for Millennials? And why are Millennials so frustrated in general? Many have a better education and are much farther along in their careers than Baby Boomers or Generation Xers were when they were the same age, so they shouldn't be so frustrated. Though this may be the case, this perspective lacks relevance. Millennials aren't concerned with how they have more opportunities and privileges than previous generations and roll their eyes when their predecessors give the "back in my day…" and "You should be grateful…" statements that lack applicability.

The idea that a joyful attitude will supplant discontentment based on the hardships of employees from yesteryear is not the case. The makeup of Millennials is different from that of previous generations and Millennials view the world through a different lens than their predecessors. This shouldn't be a surprise. Each generation has lived through a set of different social and historical events in their formative years that helped to shape their unique perspectives, diverse ambitions, and distinct views of the world. It should be expected that each generation approaches work (and life) with a mentality that doesn't always align with other employee groups.

Unfortunately, rather than indulge in the seemingly rational approach of modifying leadership techniques to meet the needs of their employees, leaders instead choose to embrace outdated tactics that served them well in the past. This needs to change for organizations to be successful. Management must leverage strategies that tap into each generation's core passions, instead of holding onto traditional approaches that worked previously.

Millennial employees operate with an entirely different perspective that conflicts with the mentality of older colleagues. To build strong workplaces, leaders must adapt their overarching management style to meet the needs of this generation. This means breaking from conformity. Fortunately, the changes required to meet the needs of this generation are many of the same changes required to be successful in the ever competitive, evolving market.

TRADITIONAL MANAGEMENT VERSUS AGILE LEADERSHIP

The Croods is a 2013 DreamWorks Animation movie about a prehistoric family whose lives are in peril after a massive earthquake destroys their home. To avoid being killed by predators, the family treks through a dangerous land in search of a new residence, much to the dismay of the overbearing, patriarchal father who is weary of change for fear of the unknown. Upon the arrival of an innovative genius filled with new ways of assessing problems and discovering solutions, a struggle for supremacy materializes as the father grows increasingly frustrated with his family's interest in following the young man's approach rather than his own steadfast way of life. After numerous close calls with death due to the inability of the father to successfully adapt, he finally sees the error of his ways and works with the prodigy to save his family and find a new home.[2]

Though this is an extreme example, the necessity of having an appropriate way of meeting the needs of your environment (and employees) is imperative. Leaders can't rest on the laurels of yesteryear, but instead must continually look for ways to evolve so that they are able to lead their employees effectively.

This isn't new. Leaders have always invested time and effort into bringing out the best in their employees. However, while the goal is clear, the ability to execute against it isn't always as apparent. Though leaders put forth their best effort to meet the demands of employees, there are times their actions are seen as outdated or less than optimal.

This makes a traditional approach toward management ineffective. Traditional management restricts how employees are permitted to do their job, only provides finite problem-solving opportunities, and limits an employee's ability to discover new ways of fulfilling their responsibilities. Additionally, traditional management doesn't instill a deeper level of engagement nor stir interest in producing excellence. It only generates short-term compliance. Millennials hate this debilitating approach! It fails to meet their needs, doesn't create passion to deliver results, and lacks the potential for them to ever be truly committed.

Millennials want *agile leadership*. Agile leadership encompasses the ability to take effective action in complex, rapidly changing conditions and deliver superior results. It focuses on balancing numerous priorities and responsibilities while being open-minded to the way each is accomplished. Leaders who leverage agile leadership empower employees to use their unique talents to discover innovative solutions, promote analyzing problems from various perspectives, and encourage members to display an intellectual curiosity.

Empower Employees to Use Their Unique Talents

Agile leadership focuses on getting the best out of employees. Knowing that no two employees are the same, leaders with an agile mentality meet employees at their current level and leverage their skills so that they can produce results.

Because employees are inevitably on different wavelengths from their counterparts, the notion that leaders can manage everyone in the same way is inaccurate. Leaders must leverage the unique skill sets of each member of the team by meeting them at their current level. This encourages both unity and individuality. Employees feel a sense of accountability to meet the demands of the job and support fellow colleagues while simultaneously continuing to grow and evolve.

Additionally, empowering employees to use their unique talents creates the opportunity to pull out skills and abilities that would not have otherwise been used. This produces the ability to meet changing business requirements while fostering an environment that is conducive to growth and encourages employees to develop new skills that can be applied on the job to benefit the company.

Analyze Problems from Various Perspectives

Agile leadership also trumps traditional management based on how problems are assessed. Today's work environment is more complex than ever before. This means multi-dimensional problems are now the norm and can't be solved by a small subset of the workforce. Instead, everyone must take part in addressing challenges.

In the past, top-level management was the primary (and in some cases only) problem solvers for companies. Leaders would often be called upon to handle issues, both large and small. Though this enabled leadership to have a strong grasp on everything that was going on, companies were often stifled because they did not assess issues from any vantage point other than that of top-level management.

In today's business environment, using this approach isn't practical. Due to the complexity of the business ecosystem and the speed at which companies operate, organizations can no longer afford to wait on a select group of leaders to analyze problems from a single perspective. Instead, everyone must evaluate challenges quickly and efficiently.

Millennials love this mentality because it connects with them on a personal level. They believe in a collaborative work environment in which everyone is valuable, and they appreciate the opportunity to participate in solving complex problems. Knowing that no one has a comprehensive view of every challenge, Millennials respect leadership that accepts different perspectives, rather than instinctively believing it has all the answers. This encourages Millennials to immerse themselves in their responsibilities.

Encourage Members to Display an Intellectual Curiosity

The final reason Millennials are drawn to agile leadership is because of their propensity to be intellectually curious. As a generation that has been inquisitive from an early age, Millennials delight in discovering innovative ways to fulfill their responsibilities. This intellectual curiosity has them maintaining a bias for challenging the status quo to find a better way to fulfill their responsibilities.

Millennials love leaders who are capable of managing through ambiguity, are willing to take calculated risks to solve problems, and are prone to developing new paths to achieve challenging goals. This liberates Millennials from confining roles. They know their leader is willing to address difficult problems in various ways.

Digging deeper, their intellectual curiosity challenges them not to rest on yesterday's successes, but rather pushes them to identify new ways to make impactful progress that will continually encourage growth. This unique balance enables Millennials to successfully manage the needs of today while simultaneously stimulating a passion for discovering what will be successful tomorrow. This openness creates the opportunity to find better ways to fulfill the mission of the company.

FIXED MINDSET VERSUS GROWTH MINDSET

People can become lulled into a particular way of thinking (or managing) that doesn't enable growth. Set in their ways, they can't think outside the box. This can easily be seen in the nine-dot brainteaser (Figure 5.1). Following are nine dots arranged in a set of three rows. Your challenge is to draw four straight lines that go through the middle of each dot without taking your pencil off the paper. In essence, the lines must be continuous, with each line starting where the preceding line finished. Try it now (turn to page 59 for the answer).[3]

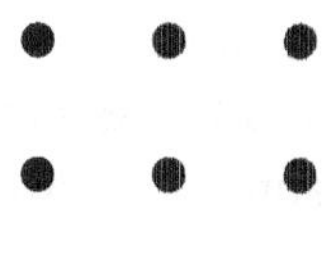

FIGURE 5.1
Nine-dot brainteaser.

Intuitively, we see the challenge in front of us and focus solely on what is inside the box because there are no dots to draw a line to on the outside. And when we fail, instead of exploring alternative ideas, looking for innovative solutions, or learning from past mistakes, we merely try the same process again and again. This approach doesn't work. We need to analyze the problem a different way.

This is often how many people used to manage their employees—a fixed mindset in which leaders did not think outside the box. They believed employees had basic abilities, intelligence, and talents that were fixed traits. Employees were responsible for a particular job and they executed against that responsibility. While employees would traditionally make small changes that would improve productivity, it was rare that exceptional modifications would occur based on employees taking overzealous initiative. Though there were a select few who would be on the forefront to facilitate large-scale transformations, these members were typically within leadership or on certain teams that specialized in these activities. This way of thinking stifled productivity and capped potential, as a distinct differentiation was made between those who were granted access to make changes and those who were not.

Conversely, most companies in today's workplace want to instill a *growth mindset*. They actively encourage employees to find better ways to do their jobs and push people to draw on their unique skills to improve the enterprise. Employees are encouraged to pursue personal and professional development. It is not enough for employees to merely do their job, fulfillment comes from helping the corporation improve.

This mentality ultimately promotes employees having an increased interest in producing results due to the palpable growth in responsibility. No longer can employees state that they are not accountable for facilitating change, require a promotion to do certain work, or need management approval for benign activities that fall outside of their traditional role. The success of the company falls on the shoulders of everyone!

Millennials love this approach. Instead of a stagnant ideology toward improvement that relies on a select few, challenging everyone to support growth makes it a shared responsibility and helps the organization flourish. This encourages the freedom to explore, endorses a learning culture, and promotes a collaborative approach toward success.

Encourage Freedom to Explore

A fixed mindset stifles productivity. People are responsible for one job and one job only. Execute against your tasks and fulfill the responsibilities within your job description, and move on, nothing more nothing less. This is painful for Millennials who want the freedom to explore. Having seen members of their generation start and lead multibillion-dollar companies, Millennials inherently want to be self-directed and have autonomy in their daily lives. Simply falling in line and following orders just won't cut it.

A growth mindset encourages exploration and provides Millennials the liberty to respectfully push boundaries and question the norm so that they can improve enterprise results. It also creates resourcefulness when faced with unforeseen obstacles. Rather than being paralyzed when something abnormal occurs, employees are able to think outside the box to find a solution.

This flexibility promotes autonomy and strengthens problem-solving skills. While Millennials who work in a controlling environment are often afraid to make decisions for fear of reprisal, Millennials in an environment that empowers employees and promotes development do not concern themselves with being penalized for ill-fated choices. They know their ingenuity is valued when they look for ways to improve the company.[4]

Endorse a Learning Culture

While a fixed mindset can endorse a learning culture, quite often it is based solely on career advancement or courses that employees must take due to company policy. This goes against the very nature of Millennials. As the first generation to grow up with endless information via the Internet, it isn't surprising that these employees are interested in acquiring knowledge in a variety of areas that fall outside of their career path. Millennials are hungry to learn and eager to expand their knowledge base both inside and outside of their career field, industry, and functional area.

This enables them to gain an understanding for all parts of the business and empowers them to see the enterprise more clearly. Instead of being fixated on their responsibilities exclusively, they acquire a big picture mentality that enables them to appreciate how they fit into the company landscape. This provides Millennials the opportunity to display intellectual curiosity, especially during struggles or failure. Instead of dwelling on mistakes and burying their heads in shame, Millennials take what they have learned and look to apply it in the future.

Endorsing a learning culture also strengthens the organization as a whole. Employees who seek to acquire knowledge and strengthen their skills not only improve themselves, but also improve the entire organization. This is enticing for Millennials and is a primary reason many gravitate toward job shadowing and cross-training opportunities. They are interested in having skills in a variety of areas and want to learn about diverse topics that fall outside of their career path.

Being seen as an expert in one area isn't enough for members of this generation: they want to be well-rounded employees capable of adding value in a variety of ways. Though this could be seen as counterproductive in the past, employees with this mentality bring with them a huge competitive advantage. Because companies face increasingly complex problems that pierce through numerous departments, having employees who possess knowledge in a variety of areas can be extremely beneficial.

Promote a Collective Approach toward Success

Finally, having a fixed mindset places responsibility for success solely on leaders. Though employees are part of the process, they look at their roles as finite and accept that they ultimately provide minimal value compared to their superiors. They are just cogs in the company wheel.

Alternatively, a growth mindset instills a sense of accountability in everyone in the organization and empowers employees to capitalize on new opportunities while challenging them to continuously innovate and improve. In a growth mindset company, everyone is a leader and merely following the path of the person in front of you is unacceptable. Employees gain a sense of ownership when a growth mindset is in place as broader perspectives toward success fill the organization and employees inspire one another.

Instead of waiting for someone else to take the initiative, employees proactively analyze business issues and prioritize how to address challenges from various angles. This creates synergies that are critical to succeeding beyond targeted outcomes and contributes to the performance of every team. Members possess a vested interest in contributing to the success of the organization. This builds the morale of everyone in the organization, because members identify as a group working together to accomplish a mission, rather than individuals responsible for merely fulfilling certain roles.

By being accountable for company success, employees naturally recognize their strengths and weaknesses, and learn how they can best deliver value to the organization. This approach enables Millennials to acknowledge both where they excel and their limitations, providing them a unique understanding of how they can add value and where they should pull from their colleagues. This ultimately places responsibility for success solely on their shoulders, and empowers them to acquire the resources, information, and support needed to execute their job and help fulfill the mission of the company (Figure 5.2).

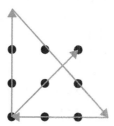

FIGURE 5.2
Solution to the nine-dot brainteaser.

BUSINESS SILOS VERSUS A COLLABORATIVE CULTURE

It was a terrifying ordeal! Having just come home from a day at the zoo, the young boy couldn't have prepared himself for what he was about to experience. Sitting in the backseat as his mother pulled into the driveway, she turned to him and said, "The lion is in the middle of the garage, get out and move him." Horrified and feeling as though his life was about to end, the 6-year-old began to weep while envisioning a mammoth creature waiting to devour him as soon as he got out of the car. He didn't know it at the time, but his mother was referring to the toy lion she gave him at Christmas.

When we don't have all of the information, we can be at a great disadvantage.

Previous generations believed that the need for collaboration and sharing information was limited. While a handful of jobs required certain employees to work together, the overwhelming majority of personnel did not need to know what their colleagues sitting in the next row over were doing on a consistent basis. Their only focus was to fulfill their responsibilities. This led to an increase in bureaucracy, duplication of work, and failure to capitalize on synergies. Instead of being able to find the best solution for issues collectively, employees were required to go to great lengths to proactively acquire information.

To make matters worse, this frustrating realization was globally accepted because it brought stability. Companies believed that having clearly defined roles in which employees did not meander outside of their specific job function would minimize confusion and reduce the potential issues that might arise. While some communication between departments and individuals could be beneficial, it wasn't as important as having a structured foundation that limited cross-functional interaction. Because of this, innovation moved at a glacial pace, with the process for implementing change being extremely arduous.

While many thought this approach was tedious, it wasn't necessarily the end of the world. Everyone was doing it. Business silos were universally accepted. Departments didn't share information, teams didn't work with one another to solve problems, and people didn't cross the aisle to discuss what others were working on. Instead, everyone worked independently or within their small cohort. Not surprisingly, as operational activities within businesses became more complex and employees began having turf wars about who was responsible for what, things got progressively worse.

The difficulty business silos created became even more of a challenge as multidimensional projects became the norm. Complexities within the work environment and departments that had only a small fraction of the required information created unnecessary challenges that led to increased dysfunction.

This made it no longer just about business silos and respecting each department's role within a company. Instead, it focused more on unhealthy competition and consistent battles for who could get the most coveted information, and how they could use it to their advantage. Rather than openly share information outside of their silo, employees held onto important material for fear that sharing might cause them to lose their own value in the company or cause people to second guess their every move. This tired approach toward business created a zero-sum game as departments (and employees) fought over information and resources, while refusing to help others.

Millennials do not understand this mentality. They love sharing information and value the opportunity to connect with colleagues. They understand that a collaborative culture enables them to have more of an influence on their peers while simultaneously strengthening the organization. In essence, it strengthens their ability to be more influential and promotes their unique interest in developing a diverse skillset. More specifically, three primary reasons Millennials value collaborative cultures are because it builds trust and allows people to see issues from various perspectives, fosters positive energy and eliminates complacency, and streamlines interdepartmental projects and cross-functional responsibilities.

Build Trust and Allow People to See Issues from Various Perspectives

When people work for an extended period of time at a company that has business silos, they often develop a considerable distaste for anyone who is not part of their group or department. This typically stems from their lone vantage point and lack of appreciation for why other parts of the company function the way they do.

Operations employees hate marketers because of the endless promises they make, never mind the business they bring in; frontline managers despise human resource personnel for always getting their people in trouble, forgetting that the policies employees are required to follow are there to maintain order; and the finance department can't stand all the money that is wasted by the research team, even though cutting-edge products bring with them exceptional returns that could not be achieved if not for the work that the research team does.

Not surprisingly, in a business with silos, employees fail to understand the importance of other departments. Their perspective remains tilted as they see other groups as the enemy that causes their altruistic mission to go askew. Clearly this is anything but true.

Collaborative cultures help employees see the importance of other departments and the value they deliver. Instead of being frustrated by the hurdles that are in the way, employees are able to effectively dialogue and discuss issues that are affecting them. This enables members from different departments to discuss why certain activities are taking place. It also creates the opportunity to analyze situations from various perspectives.

Millennials are drawn to collaborative cultures for this very reason. With an intense fear of missing out, Millennials crave having boatloads of information, and want to see how everything fits together. They enjoy learning about every part of the business and develop trusting relationships through this process.

Foster Positive Energy and Eliminate Complacency

Millennials also love a collaborative culture over business silos because of the positive energy and tremendous momentum that can be generated. When people from different departments have minimal contact with each other, it is easy to become complacent. Rather than being externally focused and driven to improve the organization, employees settle in and become satisfied with the status quo. They no longer look to improve the organization because they are only able to see a small piece of the puzzle. As stated previously, this fixed mindset is extremely unattractive to Millennials. It reduces the motivation to immerse oneself in work because of the inability to see how they are delivering value to the company.

Conversely, when a collaborative culture is present, the wide-ranging views employees possess present new opportunities. Instead of the limited perspective that members in silos have, employees in collaborative cultures are able to see the big picture and identify where they can create synergies, solve complex problems, and identify new opportunities that will be able to generate positive results. Instead of blindly guessing at what is best, a collaborative culture creates the opportunity to be at the tip of the spear and produce returns that could not be achieved otherwise.

This is easily seen by way of Research & Development communicating with the Sales Department. If R & D has minimal communication with sales associates, research employees will lack critical information necessary to understand what the end user wants, the changing preferences of the customer, and the importance of key product features that push people to buy the company's goods. Conversely, regular interaction between departments creates the opportunity to discover solutions that have the potential to deliver great value.[5]

Streamline Interdepartmental Projects and Cross-Functional Responsibilities

Finally, Millennials love a collaborative culture because it expands their breadth of knowledge and the opportunity to immerse themselves in various parts of the business. In the past, interdepartmental projects were not commonplace. Though projects often touched various departments, the initiatives did not necessitate departments becoming overly intermingled. While past generations appreciated learning about new roles and activities that fell outside of their traditional responsibilities, they were more consumed with acquiring tangible knowledge about their current job and how they could move up the corporate ladder. They did not worry about extraneous activities outside of their department.

This is different in today's workplace. While Millennials value learning about how they can grow in their careers, their inquisitive nature makes them seek more than just a promotion. Since they were young, Millennials have been able to go online and search through endless websites, view interesting videos, and discover exceptional content that would allow them to expand their breadth of knowledge. Not surprisingly, they brought this to the workplace. Millennials love the idea of being able to immerse themselves in a variety of areas and experiences. This satisfies their unique urge to elevate beyond just the next role. It enables them to explore, discover, and learn.

From a business standpoint, interdepartmental projects and cross-functional responsibilities are now the norm. Business operations are more intertwined than ever before, making it imperative to champion a collaborative culture in which everyone is able to work together.

MAINTAINING STATUS QUO VERSUS EMBRACING CHANGE

We are all guilty of it at some point—driving 85 mph on the highway, while zipping past cars and navigating around semitrucks as we cuss like a sailor at every vehicle in our way. Then suddenly, we spot a police officer tucked behind the brush on the side of the road. Caught red-handed, we immediately hit our brakes, set our phone down, and put both hands on the steering wheel, while quietly praying for a second chance.

Unfortunately, less than two minutes later we look in the rearview mirror and spot the cop with lights flashing and siren blaring headed our way. As the lump in our throat gets bigger and bigger, we think of the excuse we will give the police officer on why we were driving so erratically. At that very moment, the cop flies past us en route to another vehicle.

Feeling fortunate, we take a deep breath and set our cruise control to the speed limit, vowing that we have learned our lesson.

Yet four minutes later, we are at it again.

This is a lot like how many of us embrace changing our management style. We only focus on modifying our approach when there is a glaring problem, and once that problem disappears, we suddenly revert back to our old mentality. This philosophy must change. Leaders must be proactive, execute on their vision, and be unrelenting in their focus.

Proactive Leadership

Reacting to situations as they come is fairly common. As unforeseen issues arise, you must address them. While in some instances you have no choice but to react, there are other times that this is not the case. Just like the driver in the story, the opportunity to use an alternative approach is available. Unfortunately, an alternative approach is often viewed as unacceptable until there are no other options.

This ill-fated mentality is how many leaders manage Millennials. Though leaders know they should be more proactive and not accept a stagnant philosophy toward bringing out their best work, they choose to take the easier path and avoid being assertive. This approach remains until dire circumstances are upon them—when the results of engagement surveys are down, performance reviews are coming, or numerous Millennials suddenly depart the company. Only then do they embrace change. Unfortunately, much like the driver who almost immediately reverts back to old habits, interest in keeping the new management philosophy is short-lived due to long to-do lists and fleeting memories. Priority shifts back from a progressive leadership style and toward the old approach.

To successfully bring out the best in Millennials, proactively embracing change must be a leader's first response, not a last resort. Leaders can't use archaic methods of management to motivate Millennials; instead they must be proactive and adapt to their environment. Only by doing this will Millennials fully buy into the company's mission.

Execute on Your Vision, Don't Just Talk about It

Deliberating over proposed changes in the work environment can be interesting and discussing unique opportunities to bolster productivity is often enticing, but none of that matters to Millennials. They want action.

Millennials live in a fast-paced world in which change is happening all around them. They are not interested in merely having a long discussion or theoretical talk about how you will embrace change. They want you to execute on your vision.

Additionally, they are not content with gradual changes that slowly make their way into the workplace. While this was acceptable in the past, methodical approaches are now seen as resistance-management initiatives that will disappear shortly after being started. While this is often off base, many employees have grown accustomed to managers taking an initial interest in making change, that is abruptly abandoned shortly after no traction has been made.

If there is an exorbitant amount of discussion with little to no action, Millennials grow increasingly discontent and begin to believe that no change is forthcoming. To get and keep buy-in from Millennials, executing on your vision is imperative!

Be Unrelenting in Your Focus

While managers are able to incorporate new strategies and unique techniques to bring out the best in Millennials, all must tweak their process in some form or fashion. No one gets it perfect the first time. This can lead to frustration for many, especially those who are doing everything they can to bring about change in their company.

When this happens, the inclination to abandon new techniques could fester. Do not give in to this temptation. Instead, build on successes and use disappointments as lessons learned. This will provide you the best opportunity to adapt processes until you find what works. Managing employees isn't an exact science and finding the perfect formula isn't easy. Continue to be fluid in your approach as you look for the best way to manage Millennials.

BRINGING IT ALL TOGETHER

An unmistakable reality for every industry and market is that business is always changing; nothing stays constant and the need to continually evolve is always present. This idea is scary. Traveling down a consistent path with predictable results enables us to feel comfortable. We seemingly know what to expect. While this can work for the short-term, it is not sustainable in the long run. The truth is more complicated than that.

To be successful, businesses (and leaders) must adapt their methodology to meet the demands of the current business environment and employees in the workplace. Companies must transform processes and modify approaches toward management to maintain a competitive edge. This has never been more important than it is today. Changes in the business world are happening faster than ever. If you romanticize the past, purposely delay changes that will improve operations, or fight against the natural progression of business, you will lose. Constantly adapting to meet the needs of the current business environment and your employee-base is necessary to succeed.

ENDNOTES

1. M. Judge, dir. *Office Space*. 1999. Los Angeles, CA: 20th Century Fox, 2005. DVD.
2. C. Sanders and K. Demicco, dir. *The Croods*. 2013; Universal City, CA: Universal Pictures Home Entertainment, 2013. DVD.
3. Infinite Innovations Ltd, Creative thinking puzzle number 1—The nine dot problem to help you "think out of the box," *Infinite Innovations Ltd*, last modified March 4, 2018, http://www.brainstorming.co.uk/puzzles/ninedotsnj.html.
4. A. Zern and M. Caldwell, *Leading with a Growth Mindset* (lecture, Advanced Care Scripts, Orlando, FL, 2017).
5. J. Kotter, Breaking down silos, *Forbes*, last modified May 3, 2011, https://www.forbes.com/sites/johnkotter/2011/05/03/breaking-down-silos/#4eb64aac63b6.

6

Uber, Lyft, Airbnb, and Millennials

Short-term automobile transportation services have been dominated by taxis for over 100 years. While competition such as limousines and buses get a small piece, the lion's share of business has always gone to taxis. Similarly, hotels have been around for centuries, and have always been the primary provider of temporary lodging for travelers away from home. Similar to taxicab services, the hotel industry has always faced some competition, including resorts, hostels, and bed-and-breakfast hot spots, but in the end, have always come out with the majority of the market.

Because they never had legitimate foes, these two industry leaders became complacent. Taxi companies sent out cars that were dirty and old, charged passengers expensive rates, and had drivers who worked long hours for a low wage. Similarly, hotels increased their costs, cut corners with hospitality, and reduced amenities while adding surcharges.

Both of these stories predictably end the same way. Large companies that had stagnant approaches toward serving customers were disrupted by innovative start-ups that thought outside the box. Uber and Lyft became prominent competitors to taxi companies almost overnight. Clean cars, fast service, and inexpensive rides provided by the two young businesses easily outperform traditional cab service. Comparably, Airbnb upstaged hotel owners from around the world with premier locations, low rates, and unique amenities like flexible check-in and checkout and free Wi-Fi.

Taxi companies' and hotels' comfort-centered disposition, in which they were unwilling to embrace the changing tides in their respective industries, cost them dearly. No longer are they the untouchable power players that only fight among themselves. Instead, formidable competition outside of the traditional landscape has taken a considerable chunk of the market, with no signs of slowing down. Instead of being agile and willing to adapt, the conservative approach taken by these industry leaders cost them their competitive advantage.

This is a perfect example of what inflexible companies that do not place emphasis on what is most important will experience if they are not willing to adapt their operations. It also aligns very closely with the perils of failing to modify your leadership style to accommodate Millennials.

While it is clear that there are stark differences between these start-ups and managing Millennials, and the focus of effective business strategy versus successfully leading people is very different, the same overarching concept is present: failing to meet the needs of the market (or your people) can lead to devastating results. A rigid philosophy filled with an unwillingness to change leads to the deterioration of any competitive advantage or successful management strategy. This can be seen in every part of the dynamic disruption these companies made in their respective markets and in the way Millennials affect the workplace.

TECHNOLOGY AND INNOVATION

Technology and innovation are quite simply the reasons Uber, Lyft, and Airbnb became legitimate forces in their respective markets. Taxi companies and hotels relied on outdated methods of attracting consumers that lacked sophistication and uniqueness. Taxicabs were traditionally dispatched to a person's location after the company received a call or cars were strategically placed in highly populated areas as they waited for passengers. Though people would use a taxi if easily accessible, the simplicity of contacting Uber or Lyft through an app on a smartphone and tracking the vehicle's path is far superior.

While hotels worked to remain up-to-date with technological advances by allowing customers to reserve rooms online and using third-party vendors to fill vacant space (i.e., Hotwire, Priceline, etc.), their success was thwarted by Airbnb's innovative business model that prioritized preeminent locations, low cost, and household amenities. Though the hotel industry was leaning forward with technology, Airbnb's pioneering approach was able to steal market share. Easily sorting through each property and communicating directly with hosts created an allure that far exceeded hotel websites and third-party vendors.

These issues align with the challenges Millennials have with companies when they do not incorporate technological advances and innovation in the workplace. Stagnation kills a Millennial's drive due to the inherent awareness that the company is not putting forth effort to get better, but rather is willing to accept using archaic technological resources and outdated operational activities. With their intrinsic desire to evolve and advance, this goes against everything a Millennial stands for. They despise the seven most expensive words in business, "We have always done it that way."

If you truly want to keep Millennials in your organization, technological advances and innovation are critical. Millennials live for technology and innovation, and want it in every part of their lives. This extends beyond just social media, streaming videos, and texting with friends. They use it for banking, setting up reservations for dinner, working out, and even going to church. With this understanding, it is ridiculous to believe that they would willingly accept not incorporating technology and innovation in the workplace.

TEAMWORK AND COLLABORATION

The approach Uber, Lyft, and Airbnb took to orchestrate successful businesses relies heavily on active participation from both seller and buyer. This model is far more personal than traditional cab companies and standard hotel chains. Cab companies send random drivers to pick up passengers after a phone call is put into a call center. This detachment is often supplemented with a physical barrier between driver and passenger. Instead of a natural environment in which the two can exchange pleasantries, thick glass separates the driver from passenger, ultimately leading to awkward conversation that is difficult to maintain; the "us" and "them" mentality is clearly defined.

Conversely, after being summoned by a rider, the name and picture of the Uber or Lyft driver is prominently displayed on the rider's smartphone with a description/picture of the car. With strict standards for vehicles and drivers with a vested interest in delivering a quality experience, cars are kept in pristine condition with spotless interiors. And unlike uncomfortable conversations with taxicab drivers, Uber and Lyft drivers intuitively engage passengers. As active members of the community who know all about the area and are willing to give advice about hot spots in town, they are more than ready to provide suggestions on interesting places to visit. This has passengers actively seeking out conversation with these drivers while sharing stories and experiences of their own as value is exchanged. It is not a burden for driver and passenger to engage each other, but a pleasant dialogue in which each side can be a resource for the other.

The hotel industry has a primarily static approach toward teamwork and collaboration as well, much to the chagrin of visitors. Check-in starts at 3 p.m., extra towels are located at the pool, housekeeping will come in sometime during the day to make the bed, and the breakfast buffet runs from 6 to 10 a.m. Though the front desk is open 24-7 to provide help, there is a fairly standard approach to operations and very little interaction beyond what is expected.

Alternatively, Airbnb is all about teamwork and collaboration from the onset. The host posts a description and pictures of their place on the Airbnb site, while potential guests view the property and reach out to the owner to ask questions. Because each property is a private residence, there is no standard approach toward rentals. Instead, each guest determines what his or her needs are and chooses a property that meets those specific criteria.

Special needs that are outside of the norm are often discussed between host and guest, such as local hotspots and unique amenities that wouldn't be available in a standard hotel. For example, during a stay at an Airbnb, a couple wanted to enjoy a night out on the town but couldn't because they were unable to secure a babysitter for their two young children. Rather than accept the disappointing circumstances, the couple asked the hosts. The retired couple gladly accepted the offer and created a friendly, safe environment for the little ones while Mom and Dad went out.

Millennials were the first to use these start-ups. They love teamwork, value collaboration, and were excited to invest in the innovative businesses that promoted a communal approach.

This is how Millennials approach their jobs as well. They understand that the whole is greater than the sum of its parts, and the collective strength of the entire workforce is more potent than individuals working alone. They actively pursue teamwork and collaboration because of the opportunity to use everyone's unique skills. Instead of being isolated and working alone, they enjoy the sense of community at their workplace.

COMMUNICATION MEDIUMS AND SHARING INFORMATION

Beyond hailing a cab in the street by raising your hand and yelling "Taxi!" a phone call is the typical way riders request a cab. During this time, most taxi companies provide passengers a ballpark estimate as to when the driver will be on site. Not surprisingly, this lack of awareness as to when a passenger's car will actually show up results in frustration, anxiety, and numerous calls back to the station.

Uber and Lyft created a far superior model, with passengers able to track the driver's course from the time they request a ride to the moment they are dropped off at their end destination. This transparency provides peace of mind, as riders are capable of monitoring the entire trip. Further, to reduce almost any state of uncertainty, an estimated arrival time is provided that gives passengers a basis for when they will make it to their location. And if there is ever a case in which you need to reach out to a driver prior to them picking you up, the passenger is able to call them directly.

Airbnb offers similar benefits over hotels. Hotels traditionally offer bland messages on their website filled with stock photos that do not provide a lot context for what the guest can expect. Generic pictures of the room, pool, and exercise area leave prospective visitors lacking a profound understanding as to what their experience will actually be like.

Conversely, Airbnb pages are unique. Elegantly crafted messages about the extraordinary property and all the amenities it has to offer, and perfectly cropped pictures that highlight every part of the home leaves little doubt as to what the renter will be getting. And if there ever is a concern with the property, direct communication via email can take place with the owner/property manager. This is far superior to speaking with a call center representative or front desk clerk who has little reason to help you.

This mentality is similar to the way progressive companies leverage communication mediums and sharing information. Much like Uber, Lyft, and Airbnb took advantage of effective communication mediums and sharing information, so too is it beneficial for companies to do the same. Millennials have an unrelenting desire to actively engage others every chance they get. Face-to-face, text, email, IM, and social media all play into their extreme interest in communicating with others and their never-ending FOMO. By promoting transparency within the organization and communicating through multiple mediums, Millennials possess an increased focus on their jobs knowing that the company is not hiding anything. This inherently increases their motivation to produce results.

PRODUCTIVITY OVER TRADITION AND FORMALITIES

Uber, Lyft, and Airbnb capitalized on the inefficiencies that taxi services and hotels consistently had. Uber and Lyft's innovative use of technology delivered vehicles to passenger locations quicker, minimizing lag time. Though waiting for a ride may not have seemed overly troubling for some, reducing the amount of time waiting for a car allows passengers to arrive at their final destination earlier—a huge advantage for individuals who are always on the go. This is supplemented by the convenience of not having to carry around cash or pull out a credit card like you do in a cab. Instead, the passenger is automatically billed via the credit card already loaded on their phone—another efficiency baked into the Uber and Lyft business models.

Airbnb took advantage of the relaxed mentality travelers have that focuses less on structure and formalities, and more on enjoying the moment and appreciating the opportunity to vacation exactly the way they want. At its essence, hotels are transactional in nature with strict schedules to follow—breakfast ends at 10 a.m., checkout at noon, and a parking pass allows your car access to the garage. Conversely, Airbnbs do their best to provide convenience for vacationers while removing unwanted hassles. You can cook at your leisure, leave the keys on the kitchen table when checking out, and are able to park in the driveway, just like at home. Rather than spend time in a sterile room that looks exactly like every other room in the building, Airbnb guests are given the opportunity to experience an attractive alternative that includes a comfortable environment in which people are at ease.

This approach is similar to what Millennials are looking for in their work life. Why spend long hours at the office, fumble through excessive documentation for a project, and go over the same points again and again, when there is a streamlined approach that will save them time, increase their happiness, and enable them to improve their quality of life? There is no reason!

Millennials aren't interested in working late into the night at the office, spending countless hours on bureaucratic red tape, or sitting in meetings while leaders belabor irrelevant points. They hate wasting time and want to cut out activities that are painful, unpleasant, or lack value. Millennials are there to fulfill their responsibilities, then go about their lives. Anything that extends beyond this is rejected.

THE VALUE OF TIME

The cost of Uber and Lyft compared to taxicabs varies across the board but typically ranges between 10% and 50% in savings. However, that is not why these internet companies are thriving.[1] A primary challenge with cabs is time and accessibility. While there are taxis that sit in high occupancy areas (i.e., airports, business districts, nightclubs, etc.), it is not always assured you will get a cab when you need one. It is often the luck of the draw for a taxi to stop specifically for you. Additionally, though cabs will come out of a hub for a particular passenger, most travelers are not willing to accept the long lead times for a vehicle. In the "instant-gratification" world we live in, both of these options are rejected. People want to be picked up, so they can continue on with their lives.

This is similar to hotels and Airbnb. On average, staying at a hotel costs about 20% more than staying at an Airbnb. Price is not the issue here either though. Hotels' use of outdated reservation methods, cumbersome check-in processes, and delays in getting access to shared services are hardly something guests seek out.[2] Visitors would much prefer Airbnb's model: reserving properties without third-party vendors, no-hassle check-in, and direct communication with the owner for any issues or requests that could take away from their already busy schedules.

In these instances, Uber, Lyft, and Airbnb give time back to users. Uber and Lyft have drivers scattered throughout cities and towns waiting to get calls for a pickup. This reduces the amount of time passengers need to wait for a ride. Similarly, there is almost no check-in process for Airbnb properties. After getting to the place they reserved, guests are traditionally able to begin their vacation almost immediately—no long lines, excessive paperwork, or extended walks to the room with luggage in tow. Visitors can drop their bags and go.

This aligns perfectly with the Millennial mindset at work. Millennials are extremely focused on making certain their time counts with every-thing they do. They are not interested in 60+ hour workweeks stuck in the office or traveling to and from their workplace if they can avoid it. They believe the only thing that matters is producing results, and thus try to eliminate extraneous parts of the job that do not add value.

APPEARANCE AND ATTIRE

Almost all taxicabs and hotel rooms look the same. While it is clear that high-class taxi services and luxurious hotel suites bring a level of sophistication that extends beyond a standard ride or stay, the traditional look of a car or standard room is not appealing to passengers (or guests) who desire a unique experience. Passengers aren't interested in getting driven to their point of destination in a standard cab, they would much prefer being dropped off in a high-quality vehicle with an aesthetic appeal.

Similarly, though staying in a cookie-cutter room in a hotel is fine, guests would prefer visiting a unique property that has character and charm. The beautiful condo next to the park, luxurious lighthouse on the ocean, or quaint apartment tucked downtown all possess an attractive quality that extends well beyond a typical hotel room.

Millennials want a similar experience with the dress code in their workplace. They are averse to walking into the office and looking like everyone else and do not understand the need to dress up for the people they work alongside every day. Millennials want to express themselves with what they wear, show off their fashion sense, and create a distinct look by adding a unique piece of flair. They aren't interested in coming to the office in formal attire; casual clothes suit them much better because it empowers them to embrace their uniqueness more fully.

COMMITMENT TO THE COMPANY

Though there is usually no favoritism with cab companies, those who stay in hotels often choose their favorite brand so that they can accumulate points to earn free stays in the future. Loyal to a fault, frequent visitors often go out of their way to stay with their preferred vendor in lieu of a different chain. Though many people continue to use their favorite hotels, many others have gained appreciation for the flexibility of Airbnb. No longer handcuffed to a specific hotel chain, visitors embrace the property that best meets their specific needs for that particular trip. People are not subconsciously tied to a brand simply because of the rewards program they signed up for years earlier.

This aligns closely with Millennials in the workplace. Millennials are not married to the company they work for; they are comfortable moving from organization to organization. Though in the past employees accepted the need to stay with an employer for a certain length of time, this is not the case with Millennials. They are content jumping to the best opportunity unrelated to the amount of time they spent in their previous role. This freedom eliminates the potential for them to feel confined. Much like Airbnb (and Uber and Lyft), they are free to choose whatever they feel is best for their current situation.

INTANGIBLES

Taxicab companies are steeped in tradition and have followed similar processes for years. From calling for a cab, providing a specific address, and being charged by the mile, there aren't many differences from one taxi company to the next. Most hotels operate fairly similarly as well. From following specific housekeeping rules and regulations and knowing where to get fresh towels, to knowing what is served at the continental breakfast and when to check in and check out, there aren't many variations from hotel to hotel. While there have been updates to both industries (i.e., online booking), for the most part everything has remained status quo. This left a gaping hole in both industries that enabled Uber, Lyft, and Airbnb to steal considerable market share. Because of the staunch focus on tradition and inability to innovate, both taxi companies and hotels lost out big.

This runs parallel to workplaces. Tradition, work ethic, and interest in building on past successes are great, but with this mentality there is the risk of losing quality Millennial employees, not meeting employee demands of today, and failing to bridge the gap for tomorrow. Millennials are more focused on technology than tradition, multitasking than strengthening a single skill, and corporate social responsibility than squeezing the last dollar out of the customer. As such, you must modify your mindset to keep these employees in your organization.

BRINGING IT ALL TOGETHER

Based on the inability to evolve, it is no surprise that traditional taxicab companies and hotels are in a considerable battle against Uber, Lyft, and Airbnb. As perennial leaders in their respective industries who chose not to innovate, the market was primed for newcomers to disrupt both industries and bring about change.

Millennials have similarly flipped the script for companies all over the world. Unwilling to fall in line with the way their predecessors worked, Millennials function in a completely different manner. It is not acceptable to rest on the management approaches of yesteryear; companies must adapt to meet the needs of the market and their employee base.

Though it could be believed that adapting management strategies to meet the needs of Millennials is pandering to this subset of the workforce, the truth is that whenever a new generation enters the workforce there will always be challenges. Just like industries must continually evolve (or die), leaders must modify their management styles to be successful. It is not plausible to believe that any company can conduct business with the same approach they did just a few years ago. To maintain any competitive advantage, companies must leverage the unique talents of their employees, including Millennials. If they do not, they will suffer unenviable consequences, much like taxi companies and hotels are experiencing currently.

Finally, while all of these start-up companies have experienced their fair share of challenges, Uber, Lyft, and Airbnb have successfully upended the status quo. Though they made mistakes along the way, their attitude continues to be focused on disrupting the way traditional business is done by discovering more efficient solutions. So too, while no leader will employ the perfect management strategy for Millennials immediately, and there will be mistakes as you progress, taking action and trying a new approach is necessary to keep these employees.

ENDNOTES

[1] RideGuru Team, Uber vs. Lyft vs. taxi: Cost analysis across the United States, last modified 2017, https://ride.guru/content/newsroom/uber-vs-lyft-vs-taxi-cost-analysis-across-the-united-states.

[2] Priceonomics Team, Airbnb vs. hotels: A price comparison, last modified June 17, 2013, https://priceonomics.com/hotels/.

Section III

Beyond the Horizon

Providing the opportunity for the less fortunate to work had always weighed heavily on Fred Keller's heart. Keller, the founder and former CEO of Cascade Engineering, headquartered in Grand Rapids, Michigan, wanted his company to provide a way for those on welfare to get out of poverty and have a job. To make this a reality, he was interested in creating a welfare-to-career program dedicated to helping those in financial hardship.

Excited about this opportunity, Keller's first attempt involved personally walking down to the local mission to recruit those on welfare to work in his manufacturing plant. Keller brought back a group of excited individuals, with grins from ear-to-ear, finally having the opportunity to earn a living. Two weeks later, none of them remained.

So Keller tweaked his process and tried again. This time, he incorporated a formal six-month program that would instill good work habits and team skills. He even partnered with a local fast-food restaurant that would help him make this dream become a reality. None of the participants made it through.

But Keller wasn't discouraged. Instead, he reflected on what took place, treated them as lessons learned, and went at it again. Prior to his third attempt, he immersed himself in research and refocused his goals to align with long-term success. He also enlisted the help of a handful of colleagues who had expressed interest in this project, as well as state agencies, business groups, and non-profit organizations. The diverse team delivered another group of workers to the doors of Cascade.

This time it was different.

The company was prepared, and everyone involved was engaged. They developed enriched orientation procedures, made sure transit assistance was in place, and had an on-site social worker to support the program participants and bridge the communication challenges between workers and managers. Plus, employees who were not a part of the welfare-to-career program received cultural and social orientation training to enable the team building process to be fluid and the work environment to be welcoming. Keller and his team did their best to cover every type of challenge or issue that could stall this worthwhile opportunity, and this time, it worked! Of those who entered the welfare-to-career program, 95% remained with the company after the program finished.

Beyond just providing a social impact, the program produced increased profits and considerable cost savings. A case study completed by the Stanford Business School estimated Cascade's five-year savings totaled over $500,000 because of lower contracting costs, wage subsidies, and tax credits, and the program provided $900,000 in savings to the government due to reduction in monetary costs for welfare programs. It also created a new group of employees Cascade could tap into, enabling the company to further differentiate itself from competitors.

Keller's vision of helping to mitigate the poverty challenges in Grand Rapids became a reality. His passion for seeing how he could make a difference, willingness to take a step out into the unknown, and inclination to connect with trusted colleagues enabled him to create a unique program that served various stakeholders.

Rather than rest on this achievement, Keller took the knowledge he acquired from the welfare-to-career program and developed another initiative. The prisoner re-entry program helps people who were incarcerated return to the workforce and make a positive impact on society. It is yet another worthwhile venture that makes this company extraordinary.[1]

****

Fred Keller is not a Millennial, and the people he brought into his company were not Millennials. However, he faced a situation similar to what many companies face today: if you are bringing in a different type of workforce, you will only be successful if you take the time to capitalize on understanding their viewpoints, perspectives, and mentalities. Whether it is people on welfare, Millennials, or any other subset of the workforce, organizations that do not know how to successfully leverage the time and talents of their employees inevitably miss out on opportunities for increased success.

While some leaders believe that the employees are the problem, this is only true in limited instances. A failure to recognize ineffective management practices could also be what creates challenges. Unfortunately, this is often recognized too late; output has already reached an all-time low or there is a mass exodus from the company that shows no signs of slowing down. When this is the case, it is important to look beyond what has been used previously and focus on new, sustainable ways of managing.

ENDNOTE

[1] T. Fernholz, Best practices: Cascade engineering makes welfare-to-career a reality, last modified September 28, 2011, https://www.good.is/articles/best-practices-cascade-engineering-makes-welfare-to-career-a-reality.

7

SSSSHHHHHH ... Little Known Secrets

Every generation has certain characteristics, little quirks, and distinct idiosyncrasies that make it unique. There are activities that bring them great joy while simultaneously causing people from other generations to scratch their heads and wonder why anyone would participate in such activities. These culture clashes inevitably emerge when new generations enter the workforce.[1]

For example, Millennials can't understand why many Baby Boomers still read the newspaper, like to come into the office instead of work remotely, and enjoy having small talk with strangers instead of scrolling through their phones. The same can be said about Baby Boomers and their lack of understanding why Millennials take pictures of their dinner before they eat it, follow celebrities on social media, and broadcast daily activities on video for people who they don't know to view.

These unique behaviors are often what isolate different groups and limits opposing demographics from building a rapport. So, when the stereotypical 78-year-old grandmother posts a picture of herself with duck lips on Instagram, the world suddenly stops; so wildly uncharacteristic for this type of action to occur from a woman who "should" be well beyond this behavior. This "culture hacking" breaks down the stigma of certain behaviors and blurs generational lines. When members of a certain group change their behavior to align more closely with another group, people stop to take notice, appreciate the uniqueness of the action, and, in some cases, adopt the behavior as well.

This has the potential to be very powerful in the workplace if companies take the correct approach. While it is not necessarily advised for everyone to adopt practices that are uncomfortable for them, exposing people to different environments generates increased social awareness. It also creates the opportunity to leverage the passions and desires of a subset of the workforce by structuring business practices and organizational culture around what they are interested in instead of what is accepted as the norm. This creates the potential to tap into unused talent and provide members of the organization the opportunity to be more productive and increase their comfort level with those around them.

However, knowing what to do is the biggest challenge, and while certain leaders may believe they have the right idea and a handful of colleagues could provide guidance on what they think is appealing, in the end, it quite often misses the mark. This is often the case with Millennials. Many leaders inaccurately believe they understand the Millennial perspective or think they have answers to what this generation truly wants.

To ensure this doesn't occur, acquiring awareness about what is valuable to Millennials, even if their perspective falls outside the norm or fails to conform to what is appropriate for the current organizational constructs, is important. Beyond the guidance already discussed, there are other important issues not overly transparent. Following are little-known secrets Millennials have about you, themselves, and the business that could be shocking to many.

SECRETS ABOUT YOU (THE BOSS)

You may believe you have all the answers when it comes to what Millennials feel about you, or quite possibly, you could be the exact opposite, feeling as though you will never quite understand this generation's psyche. In reality, you probably fall in the middle somewhere, neither an expert nor a novice. Here are three subtle secrets Millennials have about you and your operation that will help you better understand them.

They Want You to Fire the A$$hole

Everyone knows him: he is the loud, abrasive Director who has been with the company for 20 years. He seems to have no accountability for what he says, how he acts, and why he does certain things. Though everyone else is responsible for their actions, he skates by without anyone even blinking an eye when he does something out of sorts or acts like a jerk. As a polarizing presence wherever he goes, he is proud of how he can walk into a room and be the center of attention, tell stories about the good ole days, and change the course of action for his team simply on a whim.

Though some of his colleagues (i.e., other Directors) allow for individuality and promote active participation from their direct reports, that is not how he runs his department. When he enters the room, the demeanor of his whole team is transformed. The loud, outgoing group of Millennials becomes a quiet collection of employees waiting for their leader to share what is to come. They silently wonder what is next and how he will stifle their productivity, hurt their motivation, and cripple their desire to work for the company.

He destroys the opportunity for anyone to grow, limits the prospect of members providing value, and paralyzes the department's ability to come close to reaching its full potential. The reason his employees are quiet isn't because they value his viewpoint or appreciate his perspective, it is because they have been beaten down so many times that they just stopped caring. They realize their opinion carries no weight and it is a waste of time to participate. The truth is, they hate him!

These Millennials despise this "killer of culture" and would relish the opportunity to help pack up this man's office if he should ever leave. The quiet, unmotivated group would transform into a team that is capable of producing exceptional results if they were ever liberated from the oppressive regime they are currently under, because in fact, they would be able to do their job. At their very core, they would love for you to fire the A$$hole.

Employee Benefits Have Changed and You Need to Adapt

"Who cares if your job is boring? We all started with boring jobs—
you're getting paid plenty, so put up with it until you get promoted."
"You have it so easy. We either brought our lunch or had to rush out
and back in 45 minutes. You've got this great company kitchen that
provides meals for you."
"Why do our employees need to work from home? I want them in the
office, so they will be productive. I never got to work from home, why
should they get to?"

These classic statements have been uttered time and again by leaders to Millennials. Quite often, they are said in a disparaging way to showcase how easy a Millennial's work life is compared to the endless challenges that the leaders had to suffer through. Though impossible to verify the accuracy of each of these claims, there is one single truth that Millennials all share regarding these comments: they don't care! Quite frankly, neither does the market.

Millennials don't care how good you believe they have it or the "luxuries" that they get to enjoy that you never saw. Though some will show special appreciation for the free coffee they get in the break room, hour-long lunches, and unique employee benefits that were farfetched just a short time ago, most Millennials come to look at these incentives as the norm. Comparing salaries from decades ago to what employees make now is impractical, expressing how fortunate Millennials are to have extended time off from work for lunch is irrelevant, and fighting technological advances (i.e., the opportunity to work remotely) demonstrates a disconnect from reality.

Different points in time create different social norms. Because of this, the market determines what companies must do to keep quality employees. And while certain activities could be seen as excessive or unnecessary, if other companies are adopting initiatives that are enticing, you must follow suit. If you do not, your best employees will leave, and you will lose.

Your Words Mean Nothing without Action

Leaders who consistently promise employees the world only to let them down time and again are nothing new. Though for the most part individuals who rise to high-ranking positions display great integrity, there are still others who fail to follow through on their word consistently. In some instances it can get so bad that members now fail to accept anything that is said at face value. Employees instinctively put their figurative guard up, roll their eyes, and wait for the inevitable letdown that is sure to come their way. In the past, excuses would often soften the blow, with many able to let go and move on.

This was often because of the considerable power of leaders compared to employees. Lack of transparency within the workplace made egregious acts, big or small, easily swept under the rug for fear of reprisal. This is not the case any longer. Employees have more power and are now comfortable voicing concerns if they feel slighted. Instead of just accepting that their leader isn't always forthright or that their words and actions fail to align, employees (especially Millennials) call them out and instinctively hold them accountable.

Though this can be uncomfortable, if you consistently fail to align your words and actions, Millennials will no longer look at you with esteem.

They will not be receptive to your leadership nor put forth quality effort. They will treat you as an unreliable frontrunner who is solely focused on yourself. Though this should go without saying, your words and actions must align for your employees to buy into your vision.

SECRETS ABOUT THEM (MILLENNIALS)

Millennials don't want to just float through life without extraordinary experiences, they want to get involved in everything and are interested in taking in as much as they can. Though this can often border on information overload and analysis paralysis, Millennials love seeing the big picture and being part of everything under the sun. Following are reasons Millennials are passionate about information, love seeing the big picture, and fail to maintain commitment to your company.

They Have a FOMO on Information

One of a Millennial's biggest fears is being the last to know. They love being invited to the meeting with high-powered executives, value acquiring knowledge about a new product that hasn't been released yet, and appreciate being the first to have a juicy piece of office gossip that they can share with friends. More than any other generation, they have an intense *fear of missing out!*

This shouldn't really be a surprise. Millennials have always been in the know. They grew up with the internet and have always had information at the tips of their fingers. With social media now being a primary way "important" information is shared and communicating with friends via text, email, or IM available 24-7, having the most up-to-date information becomes a source of pride for them.

However, the thirst for data doesn't end with important information. Millennials are also fixated on things that seem to have fairly nominal benefits, as is evident by them following celebrities that they will never meet. For example, the infamous Kardashians have millions of fans (often Millennials) from all over the world who track their every move. Not surprisingly, the rogue actions of each member of the family don't directly affect 99% of their followers, yet the passion their fans have for what they do every day makes it seem as though their lives hang in the balance. Though information about the family has limited value, Millennials enjoying having it.

This makes it apparent that Millennials are not just interested in important information, but rather sometimes just like having something to share. While it is clear that there are certain topics Millennials need to know about in the workplace (i.e., operational activities, changes in schedules, new products on the market, etc.), they also want updates on activities that do not necessarily affect them but are important to their psyche. This could include staffing changes, the use of new vendors, and unique programs that deliver value to the company (or environment). Regardless of what is shared, most Millennials can't imagine a life without information flying at them from every angle, and hence will always have an intense FOMO.

They Need to Be Part of the Big Picture and Not Just Fulfill a Role

In the past, employees were sometimes seen only as commodities that fulfilled a specific role. They were mere cogs in the machine that had minimal value and could be replaced easily. While they possessed talents that enabled the company to be successful, they weren't treated with distinction nor were they seen as being part of the big picture. Employees were merely there to do a specific job, and anything that fell outside of their responsibilities was irrelevant to them.

Disappointedly, there are still companies who hold onto this outdated approach. They believe personnel should solely focus on their work and not worry about anything unrelated to their daily activities. This approach destroys a Millennial's work ethic because of their inherent desire to learn how their role is important. Simply following orders and completing responsibilities is not enough for Millennials. They have an insatiable need to feel as though they are contributing to the success of the company.

This mentality aligns closely with how businesses now operate. With cross-functional, interdepartmental projects and initiatives that run across enterprises now the norm, the ability to focus solely on individual performance is lost. Now more than ever, shared responsibilities that span numerous departments and require united efforts are commonplace. This necessitates that everyone possess a basic understanding of the company's mission, where they fit, and why their role is important. Provide them information that extends beyond their role and enable them to appreciate how they bring value to the company.

They Don't Have Engaging Experiences, So They Lose Interest in the Company

When a four-year-old child walks into a McDonalds, the first thing he sees is the big, beautiful PlayPlace calling out to him; not the menu, line at the counter, or booths to sit down in—it is the jungle gym that stirs his heart. When a teenage girl heads into high school for her first day of classes, she isn't interested in grabbing a front row seat, opening her textbook, or learning what her homework assignment will be; she wants to connect with friends, post on social media, and show off her latest purchase. When a 38-year-old father of two young children goes to a bar with friends on a Sunday afternoon to watch football, he doesn't care about the ambiance, dinner specials, or pictures on the wall; he wants to watch the game.

Though the individuals in each of these examples seem to want something different, they are actually all after the same thing. They want an environment that will bring them energy. They are drawn to something that is outside of the establishment's primary reason for existence and crave an experience that they won't soon forget.

While the child does want to eat, the teenager to learn, and the man to drink, these activities pale in comparison to what they are truly after. They could just as easily trade in the restaurant, school, or bar, if there were the potential for a more captivating environment elsewhere.

This is consistent for Millennials in the workplace. Though the primary reason they come into the office is to do their job, they want more than that. They want to have an experience! A place that they can go to for four, six, eight, or ten hours every day that is engaging. Though this is not the only reason they change companies, it can be a primary driver. What is going to captivate them? Pique their interest every day? Motivate them to stay at your company? The answer: engaging experiences that will capture their interest and bring them positive energy.

SECRETS ABOUT THE BUSINESS

While Millennials do have an interest in being part of a successful business, they are also passionate about areas not related to the bottom line. This is both a blessing and a curse. Millennials are able to humanize business by not focusing solely on money, yet can struggle to accept the importance of sound financial decisions. Their unique viewpoint offers a fresh take on issues that have been around for many years.

Engaging the Entire Workforce Is the Only Way to Have Enduring Business Results

A common challenge that has been present for generations is the disproportion amounts of time leaders spend with high performers and problem employees in place of engaging the entire workforce. Stemming from the Pareto Principle, in which 80% of the effects come from 20% of the causes, leaders spend an exorbitant amount of time with a small percentage of employees while ignoring the vast majority.

While it is inevitable that certain employees will garner the majority of attention, to keep everyone motivated to produce results, you must place emphasis on engaging the entire workforce. Time and again the forgotten majority's motivation diminishes because they are not given attention from leadership. While some argue that placing emphasis on a select few employees is the best thing one can do, this strategy lacks sustainability. Top-tier workers will be promoted, problem employees will be removed, and the forgotten middle will remain with the organization as their productivity declines. Long-term success can only be generated when everyone is engaged, not just a select few.

Millennials easily recognize when they are not part of the small group that leaders place emphasis on, and are painfully aware when they are not seen as a priority. This is most obvious to them when their one-on-ones are cancelled, leaders display obvious signs of distraction when they are in their presence, or they are completely overlooked for any type of opportunity outside of their traditional role.

For members in the ignored majority, their mentality toward their job shifts. Suddenly, they are no longer willing to put forth as much effort. Instead, they quietly settle into a state of indifference while waiting for even the slightest attention to be paid to them as their productivity slowly declines. Even if they are given a reason to care again, they never recover to where they once were. This potentially volatile cycle continues to erode their motivation more and more each time they are overlooked until they eventually give up on their job due to the predictable nature of how they will be treated as second-class employees.

To avoid this, leaders must engage the entire workforce and place emphasis on everyone under them. While it is naïve to believe that you will be able to dedicate the same amount of time and energy to everyone, actively engaging the entire workforce creates a sense of community that inspires employees to work together. Even short conversations and casual connections enable members who are not the "chosen ones" to feel included and valued.

Building Sustainability Is More Important than Short-Term Profits

Businesses are designed to make money. This has been and always will be the reason (for profit) companies are created. However, how they operate and what their business processes are can vary based on how leaders choose to run the organization. In the past, it was an anomaly to take any action that did not have a direct, positive impact on the bottom-line. Money was the predominant driver for companies, and decisions were based almost exclusively on their financial implications.

These decisions became even more intensified and scrutinized as margins got tighter and competition tougher. Quarterly numbers became the essence of life at corporations of all sizes. Concern for the environment, ethical standards, and preserving resources was, at best, of secondary concern.

Millennials are more prone to long-term thinking. While interest in growing profits is still present, they are not willing to sacrifice long-term success for short-term gains. Instead, they focus on sustainability and preserving resources, place emphasis on reducing consumption and recycling raw materials, and prioritize maintaining an environmentally friendly balance of using natural resources. Millennials' passion for corporate social responsibility is equally strong. Decision-making based on financial implications and a moral compass challenges companies to look at operations from various perspectives, rather than just the bottom-line.

Though sustainability and corporate social responsibility could be seen merely as trends that are only good in an idealistic world, they can be supportive of a long-term approach. Millennials realize that interim success, though beneficial, is less important than finding solutions that breed enduring prosperity, and strive to make this a reality wherever they work. While making money will always be the number one priority in business, assessing operational activities with a more holistic approach will instill a sense of passion and focus in Millennials, and increase their desire to help the organization flourish.

Incorporating Technological Advances Is Critical

Millennials grew up with the latest and greatest technology, and had access to innovative products that piqued their interest throughout their formative years. This has created a dependency on technological advances in their professional lives to keep them interested in fulfilling their responsibilities. Quite often, they are unwilling to settle for anything but the best. This challenge can become increasingly difficult due to the speed at which advances in technology now occur.

This is easily seen when a Millennial (or frankly anyone) has to wait a fraction of a second longer for an app to load on their smartphone. Though this technology wasn't even dreamed up 20 years ago, the speed at which it now operates is often deemed unacceptable if there is even the slightest delay. As crazy as it sounds, the idea of anything less than an instantaneous response can frustrate users.

This is present for many Millennials when it comes to technological programs and operating systems in their jobs as well. Though companies often had applications that were cutting-edge just a few years ago, Millennials covet the most up-to-date platforms, and that means upgrading. They love learning how to use new technology and cherish the opportunity to immerse themselves in the best systems on the market. Though not a deal breaker for most Millennials, if their company doesn't use pioneering technological programs or the latest version of an application, they are often left less than fully satisfied.

Though Millennials understand not being able to purchase every technological resource due to financial limitations in their personal lives, they often fail to appreciate the same constraints their companies must manage. There are limitations to the number of new products, applications, and services that are financially viable for companies to use. Unfortunately, many Millennials fail to appreciate these constraints or how they fit into the big picture, and get frustrated when new programs and applications are not introduced. Ensure Millennials understand the financial burdens new IT programs cause to enable them to have a more profound understanding of the entire landscape and the company's bottom-line. This will provide them a better awareness as to why technological upgrades do not occur as frequently as they would like.

BRINGING IT ALL TOGETHER

While a lot of Millennial characteristics are transparent, there are still other parts of their psyche that are not obvious or have yet to be unveiled. This is often confusing for members of other generations who do not understand why Millennials think, act, or work the way they do. Instead of attempting to learn more, they stereotype Millennial behavior as impractical or odd, when in reality, it is just a different outlook that could prove to be extremely valuable. Do not discount their mentality outright. Instead, maintain an open mind and independently assess their approach and perspective on each issue. This will enable you to make a better assessment of each situation.

ENDNOTE

[1] C. Kadakia, *The Millennial Myth: Transforming Misunderstanding into Workplace Breakthroughs* (Oakland, CA: Berrett-Koehler, 2017), pp. 3–20.

8

Adapt or Die

In the late eighteenth century, the first industrial revolution material-ized as mechanization replaced manual labor. Mass extraction of coal and the invention of the steam engine created a new type of energy that transformed the way businesses operated. Productivity spiked for many industries throughout the world. This was most evident in the agriculture industry. The McCormick Harvesting Machine Company developed a new tool with a unique whirling reel of wooden bars with a sharp blade. While initially ridiculed by farmers for the contraption, McCormick's new tool increased collection of grain by a factor of six, bringing an end to hours of tedious fieldwork, while simultaneously encouraging the invention and manufacture of other innovative farming equipment. The agriculture industry was never the same.[1]

One hundred years later, at the end of the nineteenth century, the second industrial revolution was underway. Technological advancements created the emergence of new sources of energy. Oil and gas were now highly cov-eted natural resources and spurred the development of the combustion engine and rise of the automobile. A crowning achievement for this era was Henry Ford's use of the assembly line, which ultimately transformed manufacturing.

A third revolution began in the second half of the twentieth century with the emergence of a new type of energy that far surpassed its predecessors, nuclear energy. This revolution also witnessed the rise of electronics, tele-communications, and computers. These advances led to the development of miniaturized material that catapulted the implementation of complex automation in production, reducing manual labor while simultaneously improving speed and accuracy.

Today, a fourth revolution is ongoing. Led by the emergence of the inter-net, fast-paced technological advances, and digitalization, the entire world is becoming connected. Businesses are able to optimize use of production tools, track resources more effectively, and analyze data with more precision. This provides the ability to anticipate customer purchases, improve decision-making in real time, and customize orders based on predictive analysis. These enhancements have led to an entirely new way of doing business and makes competitors who do not leverage these techniques obsolete very quickly.[2,3]

Change can be difficult, and many people fight it regardless of their circumstances. It is much easier to remain in one's own comfort zone than to have to worry about pivoting in a new direction. Unfortunately, in business one does not have the opportunity to take this approach. No industry remains the same forever, no company is the market leader permanently, and no business can be stagnant and succeed. Though an organization can work hard and put forth great effort to reach the top, if they do not adapt, they will not remain relevant for long. This is evident through the many iterations within the four industrial revolutions and is applicable for workplaces as well. Business is always changing, and if you do not adapt, you will die.

To compound this challenge, change is now occurring faster than ever; nothing is the same as it was even a decade ago. For example, in 2008 a GPS was on the windshield of every car, USBs were the best way to transfer data from computer to computer, and the BlackBerry was quickly gaining prominence as the best smartphone that everyone had to have. The amazing changes that have occurred in just the past 10 years make it no surprise that the ability to rest on the successes of the past is gone. Companies must constantly modify their core business processes to keep up with the times.

While everyone in the business world is affected by change, some are able to adjust more easily than others. For those who struggle to adapt, it is necessary to accept that the market doesn't care who you are or what you want. The market will determine which products are best, how much a service is worth, and where the value in goods rests, as well as when a product no longer serves a valuable purpose. If you do not accept this, your business will suffer.

Failure to change business processes and management strategies will also lead to considerable challenges. Adapt and you will live, fail to change and you will die. Following are numerous parts of the business ecosystem that have changed in recent years. These changes require companies and leaders to adapt as well.

TECHNOLOGY AND INNOVATION

Technology and innovation are critical components of business that are endlessly going through rapid change. Thirty years ago, technology was an afterthought. While companies invested in technological advances and ways to improve operations, other aspects of the business were far more prominent. In today's work environment, technology is a part of every business decision, with the chief technology officer's opinion carrying significant weight with every decision made. Though this is universally accepted as true, how it affects the workplace is not always understood.

Specifically, every profound technological advancement is accompanied by behavioral changes as well. New technology programs or adaptations to business operations never stand alone. Instead, they always go hand in hand with changes in the way employees work. This invariably creates stressors in the organizational environment as workplaces must modify operational activities, practices, and traditions. Though these activities typically create value, there are always bumps along the way.

This challenge is even more daunting due to the speed at which everything occurs in today's business world. In the past, change occurred at a glacial pace. It would take years, sometimes even decades, for change to affect global markets. This enabled companies to embrace innovation in a controlled environment without undue stress. Conversely, in today's economy change is fast and dynamic, with markets, technologies, and products being in a constant state of flux. Everything is moving faster than ever![4]

Companies feel like they are being held hostage. Their employees are just getting comfortable with their current state of technology, but they know they should leverage the functionality of new versions of software.

Though it can be appealing to avoid technological advances and innovation due to organizational and financial hardships, to maintain competitive advantage and keep Millennials, change is necessary. New programs bring simplified operations, less labor, and cutting-edge service. The unwillingness to upgrade technology or incorporate revolutionary processes for an extended period of time will inevitably push quality employees away while simultaneously not enabling you to keep up with the competition.

CHANGING COMMUNICATION MEDIUMS

The mechanism used to communicate messages between sender and receiver has invariably changed from the beginning of time. From hieroglyphics and smoke signals, to mailing letters and land-lines, to apps on cell phones and virtual reality, the platform for how information is communicated constantly changes. While the medium used for how people communicate never stops changing, how certain groups of individuals prefer to communicate often depends on their generation.

This can be a problem, especially for older generations. Though the use of the spoken word will never be completely removed from business communication, its prominence has faded because of the speed at which businesses operate in today's workplace and endless responsibilities employees must complete. High-tech alternatives are preferred due to the ease at which information can be shared. Employees, especially Millennials, love having the opportunity to communicate with numerous people through multiple channels at the same time. Many employees typically prefer leveraging the technological resources available to them over face-to-face interaction.

Be open to using various communication methods, and don't limit yourself to a specific platform just because it is comfortable. Instead, place emphasis on where everyone's attention is focused. The importance of using appropriate mediums can easily be seen in how marketing campaigns have changed over the years. Specifically, though companies were inherently used to advertising in newspapers and promotional flyers, over the course of time radio and television became the primary means of promotion. This trend remained consistent for decades until recently, when the advent of digital marketing became the best way to engage audiences. People who continue to use outdated marketing methods invariably miss out on attracting customers because of the inability to change along with the market.

This aligns closely with how businesses should communicate. Focus on where everyone's attention is, not necessarily what your preferred method is for that specific situation. Leveraging the resources available to you is far more important than merely going with a specific medium that is comfortable.[5]

SMARTPHONES, SOCIAL MEDIA, AND SHARING INFORMATION

In the past, when employees went off to work, rarely was there contact with the outside world. Though on occasion employees would receive a phone call or have the opportunity to watch television during lunch, typically they didn't have the ability to communicate with family and friends or catch up on current events. When employees left for work, they did not communicate with loved ones, nor did they have a lot of awareness with what was going on in the world.

In today's workplace, everyone has a smartphone, and most are texting with family and friends, scrolling through social media, or brushing up on current events throughout the day. These distractions can be devastating for productivity, with some employees spending more time on their phones than their responsibilities. This shouldn't necessarily be surprising. Whether we like it or not, downtime in the workplace always exists, and when downtime is present, employees instinctively reach for their phones.

This aligns closely with the actions most people take in their personal lives. During discretionary time people are inevitably on their phones, regardless of where they are and what they are doing. This behavior reaches its ultimate uniqueness when Millennials are watching television. During commercials, the uniform reaction of almost every Millennial is to instinctively check email, scroll through social media, or text with friends. If their impulse during discretionary time is to use their phone, it is hard to imagine that while at work they will not take the same approach.

This trend will not go away, but rather increase. More obligations, commitments, and extracurricular activities create the need to multitask whenever possible, and that includes while on the job. Any possible way to blend personal life with professional responsibilities will be done.

Though everyone should remain focused while on the clock, attention redirected toward personal life is natural. This occurs at every level of employee, from frontline personnel to C-Level leaders. While you may try to curb this behavior, leveraging the benefits could be more beneficial, especially because it would lack integrity to hold employees accountable for rules that leaders themselves do not follow. While different rules and policies must be developed based on industry and function, for many roles the impact of texting with friends or scrolling through social media will have minimal effects. If employees are able to fulfill their responsibilities, there is no reason they shouldn't be able to use their devices on the job.

Instead of reprimanding employees, take a more active approach for sharing information. In the past, almost all information was held close to the vest, with only certain people being privileged to learn about product developments, new projects, and upcoming changes to the business. This has changed. The world has become a more social and inclusive community. Take advantage of the unique interest that employees possess and actively encourage them to share information about the company.

Specifically, provide employees access to information that can be posted or shared quickly and easily. Give them the opportunity to brag about their workplace or highlight upcoming events that the company is going to be hosting (e.g., an upcoming sale). Easily accessible messages that enable members to openly share about the company flips the script. Suddenly employees accessing their phones won't be looked at so negatively. While it is clear this can't be used in every industry and job, and employees will inevitably place emphasis on their personal lives over work, by providing a simplified approach to sharing information, smartphones can suddenly generate a buzz rather than just be a distraction.

WORKING IN A REMOTE ENVIRONMENT

It was once true that everyone had to come to the workplace to be productive. This is still the case for many industries. However, when it is feasible for employees to do their job remotely, yet leaders continue to embrace the age-old mentality, employees look for alternative places to work. This is often because companies all over the world are allowing, and in some cases encouraging, employees to work remotely instead of drudging into the office.

Surprisingly, many leaders still react negatively to this, choosing to express the longstanding argument that they had to come into the office every day throughout their career, so it shouldn't be a problem for this generation of workers to follow suit; or that they feel more comfortable when they have everyone in the office rather than having people scattered in various locations. While both of these arguments could have merit, in the end if the market (or your competition) is allowing employees to work from home, you must adapt. If you do not, your employees will continue to navigate away from your company and toward your competition.

If there is no added value for employees to wake up early, get dressed, and make the commute into the office, why would they continue to do so instead of making a change? What rationale is there for them to blindly continue working for you when competitors within the same industry allow for an easier day? What intrinsic value does sticking with you have over finding something new?

The truth is that there is none.

If there is a more attractive alternative, people are going to gravitate to it. That is why you watch Netflix instead of cable, order books on Amazon rather than buy them in the store, and stop off at Starbucks for a latte in place of trying to make one on your own.

This harsh reality has grown more evident in recent years due to the ease at which people are capable of changing jobs. In the past, the ability to find work was difficult. Sifting through want ads in the newspaper, cold-calling companies, and waiting for job fairs were the primary methods for finding and landing a job. This has changed. Employees have more access to new opportunities than ever before and can change their job a lot easier. In today's world, companies post new opportunities on their websites 365 days a year. This simplifies the ability to find, apply for, and land a new position.

The market will always determine what consumers (and employees) will bear, and with many companies already providing the opportunity for employees to work from home, the notion that your staff will choose a less appealing option for similar benefits is untrue. If competitors provide the opportunity for employees to work remotely, you must follow suit.

Beyond just keeping up with the competition, providing the opportunity for employees to work remotely can be a competitive advantage. Not requiring employees to be in the office every day enables companies to enlarge their pool of talent. Talented employees who live too far away for a comfortable daily commute could refrain from applying for a job if working out of the home is not an option.

PRIORITIES IN THE WORKPLACE

The importance of developing an effective process has always held significance for many who joined the workforce prior to Millennials. Creating well-established procedures that enable the business (or employees) to follow a certain path to get to the destination desired delivered peace of mind. Many times, it was held in higher regard than actual results. Though this mentality has changed over time, some leaders still value well-defined procedures or business as usual over innovation. It is important to change these ideals.

Predominant focus on productivity enables employees to take advantage of innovation and empowers team members to create better processes and simplified operations. This goes against the very nature of many people in the workforce who are not comfortable with ambiguity and uncertainty. Nevertheless, for progress to occur, being flexible with change is necessary. There will always be bumps along the road. Instead of being rigid and inflexible, companies must now be agile and nimble to perform their best.

Beyond just changing the mindset regarding processes over productivity, companies must also alter their viewpoint on attire. Dress codes have become increasingly lax over the years, with many organizations focused on keeping things casual in the office. Though maintaining certain standards is necessary, the benefits of having employees wear clothes that are more formal (and often less comfortable) are fleeting.

While it is important to look professional, especially for important meetings, client visits, and business trips, putting excessive emphasis on business attire strays away from what the focus of the business should be—producing results. This is often frustrating for Millennials. Most Millennials have a fairly lax mentality toward dress codes and appreciate having freedom to express themselves. Though not typically a deal breaker for most Millennials, a company placing extra emphasis on proper attire is not appealing.

INTANGIBLES

Profitability is the essence of why companies are in business. However, the full cost to be successful is often debated. This argument, especially in relation to the environment, has been around for generations, and has become increasingly visible due to information becoming more easily accessible. Most notably, while in the past the environment was not a considerable issue for companies, in this day and age the focus has shifted. The environment is now a hot topic, with reducing waste, minimizing emissions, and discovering pioneering ways to reuse products all becoming top priorities. Millennials particularly care about being green and minimizing degradation of the environment. Integrating sustainability solidifies awareness that the bottom-line is not the only thing that matters.

Additionally, appropriate behavior by leadership is growing increasingly important. Scandals are not new to the corporate world, but the way information passes from one person to the next creates increased scrutiny. Never has it been easier for lewd behavior to be exposed and "go viral" via the internet. A single illicit action has the potential to destroy an otherwise pristine reputation. This requires leaders to be exceptionally careful with how they act, both in the office and outside of work.

Finally, the workplace is more diverse today than it has ever been. While in the past, cultures, ethnicities, behavioral traits, and social norms were fairly uniform across organizations, that is not the case anymore. Employees from all walks of life now fill organizations at every level. This creates the need to not only accept employees who have a different way of life, but to welcome it. These members of your team are able to identify with unique subsets of the world, creating the opportunity to have competitive advantage. Employees should not be rejected or told to "fit in" if they are different. Instead, each member of the team should be embraced and treated with distinct value.

BRINGING IT ALL TOGETHER

Success has always required change. The horse and buggy was replaced by privately owned automobiles, that in turn, have been swapped for Zipcars, Uber, and Lyft, that will soon relent to self-driving vehicles. Just as the transportation industry has changed, so too is there a need for businesses and managers to change as well. Millennials bring exceptional opportunities (and unique challenges) that were not present in the workplace previously. To produce optimal results in the workplace and bring out the best in Millennials, modifying your approach is imperative.

This is even more important in today's world due to the pace at which change is occurring. While in the past, companies had the luxury of transitioning slowly, in today's economy this liberty has disappeared. The speed at which business industries change, technologies evolve, and markets fluctuate make it clear that remaining stagnant is not an option. Instead, you must look holistically at your organization and employees, and embrace the changes necessary for your business to succeed.

ENDNOTES

[1] Fortune Editors, 27 companies that changed the world, *Fortune*, last modified June 11, 2014, http://fortune.com/2014/06/11/27-companies-that-changed-the-world/.

[2] Sentryo, The 4 industrial revolutions, *Sentryo*, last modified February 23, 2017, https://www.sentryo.net/the-4-industrial-revolutions/.

[3] A. Murray, CEOs: The revolution is coming, *Fortune*, last modified March 8, 2016, http://fortune.com/2016/03/08/davos-new-industrial-revolution/.

[4] F. Hoque, Adapt or die: Your business's only options in an evolving economy, *Fast Economy*, last modified May 16, 2014, https://www.fastcompany.com/3030618/adapt-or-die-these-are-your-businesss-only-options-in-an-evolving-economy.

[5] G. Vaynerchuk, Best business to start in 2017, online video, YouTube, https://www.youtube.com/watch?v=Q-JWAkaGQ-U.

9

We Are Managers Not Magicians

The overwhelming majority of Millennials are not the lazy, entitled narcissists the world has labeled them to be. They are incorrectly stereotyped and misrepresented. However, they do see the world differently than previous generations, maintain different priorities, and place value on different parts of their lives. Most have exceptional potential and want to use their time and talents to bring value to your company. Leveraging the skills of these Millennials will enable your organization to thrive!

While there are high-quality Millennials in the workplace, there are also Millennials who do not fall into this category—Millennials who do not want to work hard, are not interested in putting forth a genuine effort, and are always looking for the easy way out. They have labeled themselves as the new breed of employee who is misunderstood and undervalued, when in reality, they hide behind the hard work of their peers who are exceptional performers. Unfortunately, these outliers often reinforce the negative stereotypes that have gone hand-in-hand with the Millennial generation, and regardless of what you do, they will never put forth an honest effort. If you are lucky, they will eventually quit and leave your organization. If you are not, they will quit and stay.

When you come across these Millennials, remember that not all attrition is negative and losing members of the team who are not producing results can be beneficial. While it is never acceptable for employers to be rooting against employees, taking inventory of your staff to identify if certain members are a bad fit can be helpful. If this is the case, it may be advantageous to help them transition into a new role. Whether it is in a different department that will be able to better use their knowledge and abilities or an entirely new organization, a change in vocation could be what is needed for everyone involved.

However, before reassignment to a new department or removal from the organization altogether, you should analyze from a holistic view while objectively asking these questions:

- How are employees being motivated? Are outdated management techniques such as nominal pay raises, potential opportunities for advancement, and fun perks being used? Or are intrinsic motivators and intangible benefits the primary drivers of productivity, satisfaction, and retention?
- Does the Millennial align closely with a specific archetype from Chapter 3? Can you use the guidance provided to improve their performance while also holding them accountable for results?
- Is turnover rampant in your organization or in one leader's section?

Though not the only questions to ask, these inquiries will provide a deeper knowledge base for why certain Millennials are not producing results and enable broader understanding of the organization. Based on the answers to these questions and pulling from what is in this book, you can start to structure a course of action to improve performance. This will transform the work ethic, productivity, and retention of most Millennials.

However, there are slackers in every organization, so this is not always the case. While leaders of organizations can inspire greatness to emerge, managers are not magicians, so the notion that they will be able to mystically captivate a habitually subpar performer every time isn't true. Though these types of situations are never pleasant, decisive action that will correct the problem may be necessary. Reassignment to a new department that is a better fit or removal from the organization altogether could be the best course of action. While undesirable at the time, the long-term benefits will offset the temporary hardship.

Alternatively, in some situations, proper analysis will unveil that it is not the employee's fault at all. Instead, it is leadership. Just as there are employees who are not motivated to produce results, so too are there leaders who are incapable of bringing out an employee's best performance or retaining quality members of the team.

It is no secret that the number one reason employees quit their jobs is because of their manager; not poor pay, long work hours, or failure to get a promotion, it is leadership. This, coupled with the realization that recruiting, hiring, and training a new employee can cost anywhere between one and a half to three times a position's annual salary makes it no surprise that every time you lose a member of your team, it hurts.

In spite of the obvious cause and effect relationship between subpar leadership and employee turnover, rarely is anything done that fixes the problem. Instead, a group of leaders huddle together to determine the most effective way to increase productivity and retain employees. They give out pay raises, create fun programs like "Taco Tuesday," and host Friday happy hours at the local pub down the street. Surprisingly, all are disappointed that these trivial activities weren't the cornerstone to fixing the issue. And so, the Millennial conundrum continues.

The truth is, it isn't surprising that these actions don't work.

By taking a step back and looking at the entire situation, the opportunity to solve this challenge becomes fairly easy. This is primarily because of the cause and effect relationship between leaders and employee retention.

Leaders are the primary reason employees leave their jobs. Instead of looking at employees as the source of the problem, address the issue from a different vantage point. Set performance goals that hold leaders accountable for the retention of their employees. Specifically, challenge leaders to hit an annual performance goal with tangible benefits or consequences for reaching or failing to reach the expected standard. With performance evaluations, bonuses, and even continued employment tied to these scores, suddenly legitimate interest in increasing retention becomes a high priority. No longer will leaders be able to have excessive employee turnover with no consequences: instead, they will be held to a standard.

Though this will not completely eliminate undesirable employee attrition, it will create a vested interest in leaders to curb this trend and reduce the number of employees leaving their department and the organization.

BRINGING IT ALL TOGETHER

Regardless of who you are and what business you are involved in, you must clearly define standards and hold people accountable. When people successfully fulfill their responsibilities, accountability is not an issue. However, when individuals fail to meet the mark, uncomfortable conversations must take place. While this can create challenges in the short run, it will prove to be valuable over the long haul. Employees who are not producing results or causing others to be less productive do not serve the company well. Removing them from the department or organization can be the best option.

Section IV

Making Changes, Taking Action

Maintaining the status quo in today's business world won't cut it. The market has never been more competitive and the need to successfully leverage the talent in your organization and take advantage of the operational changes that are occurring in the workplace has never been more important. While broad strategies, long-term planning, and quality discussion from this book can be helpful, without taking definitive action, benefits will be limited. If you are ready to make changes, but don't know where to start, these solutions will get you moving.

In this section, there are over 100 ready-to-use solutions from 18 real-world issues designed to get the best out of Millennials. These solutions empower you to improve your business and increase productivity and profitability. To simplify this process, this section has been separated into three chapters, enabling leaders to select the proper solutions that align best with their specific situation.

The opening chapter focuses exclusively on motivating Millennials. The real-world issues discussed range from increasing Millennial loyalty and commitment to your organization to using unique ways to compensate Millennials that do not involve money.

The next chapter covers generational diversity and the challenges that come with bringing different employee groups together. Paying particular attention to issues that surface due to conflicting perspectives, this chapter provides guidance and direction for problems that cause turmoil in the workplace because of generational diversity. Leaders are provided specific actions to take to minimize problems that often disrupt harmony in the office.

The final chapter revolves around abstract challenges that are often outside of the norm for leaders. These issues do not always have answers that are intuitive for management, so are often incorrectly addressed. This chapter also uncovers many of the mysteries behind these issues.

10

Motivating Millennials

Motivating employees is an interesting challenge for companies in the twenty-first century. In the past, it was believed money was the ultimate motivator and served as the driver for improving performance. In essence, if you wanted employees to perform a certain way, you needed to increase their wage, and theoretically, the bigger the pay increase, the better the results. In reality, this approach does not carry weight. The notion that employees will chase after money the way a donkey chases after a carrot on a stick is not true.

While an increase in compensation can lead to better performance, research shows that it is only sustainable when it will generate a lifestyle change. Nominal pay raises will not create long-term motivation. So, while a small bump in pay is appreciated, to bring out enduring engagement, companies must place emphasis beyond just an employee's bank account. This is especially true for Millennials.

Companies have taken note of this and started introducing new activities to the workplace to ensure Millennials are able to produce optimal results. While some companies found great success motivating Millennials, others failed to generate inspiration. Though they are eager to stimulate employees and boost productivity, they spend time and money on the wrong initiatives. How does passing out candy, having beer in the break room fridge, or letting people wear their favorite football jersey to work create long-term motivation? Produce better results? Help employees become more engaged? The truth is, they don't! These are perks, not drivers of engagement that motivate. Yet these are the sexy activities brought up when discussions about improving productivity and increasing employee engagement surface.

Far too often, companies (and leaders) that are trying to motivate Millennials highlight the wrong activities when discussing the best ways to inspire personnel. Focus on what is important is replaced with quick fixes, fun events, and shortsighted solutions. The pinball machine in the corner of the break room and Friday happy hours are great and appear to show how innovative and trendy a company is, but they do not get to the core of why Millennials will immerse themselves in their work. It takes more than these trivial activities to captivate the Millennial workforce.

Unfortunately, while this is true, the actions necessary to motivate employees aren't always as noticeable or enticing. It is much more exciting to showcase holiday parties and Halloween costume contests. Though fun activities are more intriguing, their importance pales in comparison. Further, when thinking from a holistic point of view, appropriate analysis must occur:

- Are a couple pieces of candy really the only thing that is stopping your team from being productive?
- Is not having beer in the fridge the reason people aren't putting forth concerted effort?
- Will allowing members of your team to wear football jerseys actually inspire them?

Are we so naïve to believe that these inconsequential changes are really the cornerstone to transforming the behavior of employees and triggering increased productivity? When analyzing from this perspective, it is clear that more thoughtful initiatives must take place for Millennials to be motivated in the workplace.

The rest of this chapter comprises six issues companies commonly face and specific actions you can take to combat these challenges. Most of the actions recommended are fairly straightforward. However, others are not linear in nature and require outside-the-box thinking due to the unique perspective of Millennials. For traditionalists who might scoff at these "outlandish" ideas, the acceptance of the changing workforce due to Millennial involvement must be acknowledged. Because they have become the largest population of workers in the United States, adapting your management style to successfully motivate Millennials to perform has never been more important.

The six real-world issues discussed in this chapter are:

- Five tips for communicating feedback to Millennials
- Ten ways to compensate Millennials that don't involve money

- Five keys to effectively recognize Millennial contributions
- Ten ways to increase Millennial loyalty and commitment to your organization
- Five reasons Millennials quit and what you can do to stop them
- Five tips for motivating melancholy Millennials

FIVE TIPS FOR COMMUNICATING FEEDBACK TO MILLENNIALS

It isn't shocking to know that preferred methods of communication vary for different employees. These differences are often magnified when more than one generation is involved. Unfortunately, while many business practices have been modified to account for the vast differences in intergenerational populations, for the most part, employee feedback has remained the same. This can be particularly challenging for Millennial employees who have different preferred methods of communication than other generations. This creates the need to adapt how you communicate feedback to Millennials. Following are five tips for how you should communicate feedback to Millennials.

1. *Provide consistent feedback*: Annual reviews are not enough. While annual reviews are a part of almost every company culture, Millennials need more consistent feedback than yearly evaluations. They want to know what they are doing well, where they can improve, and how they can grow with the company on a consistent basis. Provide feedback weekly (or even daily if necessary).

2. *Be direct and to the point*: Millennials want concise communication that delivers important information. They are used to reading (and delivering) 140-character messages via twitter, so the moment you send them a 10-page detailed report about what they are doing well and where they can improve or belabor points in a long, drawn-out speech, you have lost them. Do not waste time or mince words. Written correspondence should be direct and to the point, and face-to-face feedback should be results-focused with specific action items that have tangible benefits.

3. *Provide context*: Specific examples enable abstract comments to come alive. More than just an explanation of what they are doing

well and where they can improve, Millennials want context. Provide specific examples of a Millennial's behavior, and how it positively or negatively affected the outcome of a certain situation.

4. *Expect to have a discussion, not give a monologue*: Unlike previous generations in which employees would take feedback from a leader with the mentality that "the Boss knows best," this is not the case anymore. While Millennials still respect their manager and the guidance they provide, the willingness to mindlessly trust is gone. Millennials want to share a dialogue and discuss constructive criticism to understand the leader's rationale behind the feedback.

5. *Use varied methods for feedback*: Face-to-face feedback is good, but informal feedback via email, text, IM, or even video can have the same effect. Millennials grew up in a home that had hundreds of TV channels, endless opportunities to stream videos online, social media, and constant contact via text with virtually anyone at any time. Thus, face-to-face communication may not be the best method for delivering information. While formal (annual) feedback sessions are likely to remain the same for the foreseeable future, varying the way you communicate constructive criticism informally is imperative.

TEN WAYS TO COMPENSATE MILLENNIALS THAT DON'T INVOLVE MONEY

In the past, an increase in pay was believed to be the best way to motivate employees. While financial compensation is still a motivator that can generate specific behavior, incremental increases in pay do not produce transformative performance. Specifically, while a small pay raise may have been extremely important to previous generations, many Millennials would gladly sacrifice a nominal increase in their paycheck for intangible benefits. Following are ten ways to compensate Millennials that don't involve money.

1. *Provide time off*: It could be argued that Millennials value their time more than any other generation. They love having a busy schedule, yet feel like they never have enough time to accomplish everything. This makes time away from the office well received; an afternoon

away from work enables Millennials to immerse themselves in activities that they truly enjoy.

2. *Allow them to work from home*: Similar to time off, the opportunity to work from home is also revered by Millennials. Millennials (in certain industries or roles) feel that a laptop and an internet connection are the only things they need to be able to do their job effectively. As such, when they are presented with the opportunity to work from home, they cherish the experience. This also creates awareness that you trust them.

3. *Let them stretch out in an office for the day*: Provide an outstanding performer the opportunity to use an office that is typically vacant as a reward for their excellent performance. An employee who traditionally works in tight quarters or an open workspace would appreciate the opportunity to stretch out in a nice office for a change. Alternatively, if there is no vacant space, provide the outstanding performer the opportunity to use an executive's office. High-level executives typically travel a lot. Rather than allow their workspace to go unused while they are on the road, provide the outstanding performer the opportunity to use their office as a reward.

4. *Connect them with C-Level Executives*: Millennials love rubbing elbows with the big players in the organization and would treasure the opportunity to take on a challenging project with C-Level Leadership. If a Millennial is producing exceptional results, put them on an important project with leaders of the company. This will enable them to showcase their skills while simultaneously strengthening their commitment to the organization.

5. *Recognize them on LinkedIn*: Research shows that cash bonuses are typically spent on bills and perks are soon forgotten, but recognition becomes a lasting memory that encourages exceptional performance. Recognize employees on LinkedIn. Celebrate a Millennial's contributions by formally recognizing them on their LinkedIn profile. Not only will they appreciate the kind words the first time they read them, but they will also have the opportunity to go back and read them again and again. This will provide encouragement well after you shared your sentiments the first time.

6. *Pay for a cooking, painting, or skydiving class*: Because financial compensation is spent on bills rather than an outing or

experience, the opportunity to provide high performers with a tangible reward for a specific activity could seem daunting. This doesn't have to be the case. Instead of simply giving employees a cash bonus, reward them with an activity that has already been paid for. Give high performers a gift card for a fun activity or night out on the town.

7. *Present them with a stuffed giraffe*: Quite often, certain employees will go above and beyond their responsibilities and stick their neck out for the company. When this occurs, they should be presented with an award that is emblematic of their effort. They could be given a stuffed giraffe that symbolically represents their extraordinary dedication and willingness to stick their neck out for the team. During a meeting, introduce a stuffed giraffe to your team. Share what the giraffe represents and how each month the giraffe will be given to someone who has stuck their neck out for the company.[1]

8. *Cater a breakfast for that person's team*: Celebrations are more fun when they can be enjoyed by a group of people. Instead of just providing breakfast for a single employee who is being recognized for their outstanding effort, enable that employee's team to bask in the celebration. This will enable the team member to feel appreciated by management, while also building a rapport with fellow colleagues.

9. *Send them on a field trip to a local vendor*: Seeing different parts of the industry and where your organization sits in the value stream is inspiring due to understanding how your company fits into the industry's ecosystem. When a Millennial performs exceptionally well, send them out to a local vendor. This will enable them to see how their actions make a difference and allow them to appreciate what they do on a daily basis.

10. *Write them a letter or present them a handwritten note*: Though customary in the past, the impactful activity of writing a letter to acknowledge exceptional performance has gone by the wayside. Stop to take the time to write a letter to a Millennial about their performance. This will encourage them to continue pursuing greatness. To take this a step further, mail a copy of the letter to their home address. This will inform their family what their loved one has done and why they are valued.[2]

FIVE KEYS TO EFFECTIVELY RECOGNIZING MILLENNIAL CONTRIBUTIONS

More than just compensating Millennials and creating innovative ways to celebrate success, facilitating recognition in an appropriate and timely manner is also important. Unfortunately, too often leaders have good intentions and want to recognize employees, yet fail to do so because they are uncertain how to broach the topic initially. To fight against this tendency, following are five keys to effectively recognizing Millennials.

1. *Recognize contributions as soon as possible*: Quite often, leaders have the best of intentions and are interested in recognizing employees, but fail to do so. This typically happens for two reasons: work gets piled up so they put it off for so long that they forget to recognize the employee or they wait to find the "perfect" moment to acknowledge the efforts the employee made yet never pull the trigger. To stop this from happening, recognize employees as soon as possible. Timely recognition ensures the employee understands your appreciation for their work and encourages the member to execute similar action again in the future.

2. *Be authentic*: Doling out affirmation after affirmation makes true compliments less valuable. While celebrating small successes is important, highlighting actions that do not provide value or are basic activities (i.e., celebrating employees being on time for work), reduces the effectiveness of authentic recognition. The "everybody gets a trophy" mentality shouldn't be present in the workplace. When celebrating the accomplishments of employees, make certain that you do so in an authentic manner.

3. *Celebrate the team and the employee*: It can be customary to celebrate the successes of a team rather than highlight individual performers. While acknowledging a team's performance is important, it is also valuable to recognize individual efforts. Employees inevitably deliver varying levels of productivity to projects, tasks, and deliverables. Therefore, not only is it important to recognize a team that produces extraordinary results, it is also valuable to celebrate individual performers who go above and beyond. This will encourage that specific employee to continue that behavior while also motivating others to follow suit.

4. *Congratulate in a community*: Recognizing a Millennial's contributions in private is fine, but celebrating in public is also important. This will not only encourage them to continue the same behavior, but will also motivate others to exude similar conduct. Though some may be against being publicly recognized, most Millennials have a strong social media presence, so are comfortable having their successes shared with others.

5. *Create a community that empowers others to recognize exceptional work*: Leaders can't be everywhere, so their ability to recognize quality work is not always feasible. By creating an environment that empowers others to recognize the accomplishments of colleagues, you can successfully highlight exceptional work. Whether it is a specific time during a meeting in which employees are able to highlight a colleague's actions or a page on the company website where people can recognize what their coworkers have accomplished online, creating an environment where everyone can deliver encouragement is beneficial.

TEN WAYS TO INCREASE MILLENNIAL LOYALTY AND COMMITMENT TO YOUR ORGANIZATION

Loyalty and commitment are two attributes that every company craves from its employees. More than just a willingness to show up and complete assigned duties, companies want to have employees who are completely dedicated to the organization: they want employees who will give 110%!

Money used to be the way to ensure loyalty and commitment were strong. Times have changed. In today's environment, employees will gladly trade in a job that makes more money for intrinsic rewards and intangible benefits. Following are ten ways to increase Millennial loyalty and commitment.

1. *Show them why their work is important*: Millennials want to make a difference at their job. They aren't willing to mindlessly punch a clock and work until their shift is over: they want to add value. It doesn't matter if it is their first week on the job or they have been with the organization for the past 10 years, show them how their

actions make an impact. While for some occupations this is easy, for other jobs it isn't as simple. For positions in which an employee's impact isn't easy to see, focus on how the work the employee is doing positively affects the end user or customer.

2. *Display appreciation for them that extends beyond their bank account*: Whether it is providing them the opportunity to work from home, giving them a day off, or presenting them with a handwritten letter expressing your gratitude, demonstrating appreciation that extends beyond their bank account is huge for Millennials. Display a sincere appreciation for who they are and what they do.

3. *Facilitate team-building exercises*: As simple as it sounds, incorporating regularly scheduled team-building exercises goes a long way. A primary reason involves Millennials seeing colleagues as human beings rather than mere cogs in the wheel. When this occurs, people are more willing to go the extra mile for one another, knowing that it isn't just about supporting the organization: it is about taking care of people with whom they have a personal connection.

4. *Challenge them with difficult work*: Almost every employee is interested in using their unique skills to bring value to the organization. Unfortunately, when this doesn't occur or employees fall into a routine that involves work that is not challenging, they become complacent and are more likely to leave. To minimize the risk of losing Millennials, challenge them with difficult work that requires them to grow. Though this may seem counterintuitive, by challenging employees with difficult work, they will have to immerse themselves in whatever they are doing to meet expectations. This will strengthen their resolve.

5. *Define expectations and responsibilities*: Few things are more frustrating than a manager and employee having a disconnect about what is expected from the other. While every situation is different, managers and employees must have a strong understanding of what each other is responsible for doing, to ensure ongoing commitment to the organization. Discussions about expectations could be as basic as preferred methods of communication and frequency of one-on-one meetings, or could cover intricate details involving the prioritization of projects and operational activities each member of the team is responsible for completing.

6. *Give them projects outside of their traditional role*: Millennials love having numerous things going on. Whether it is personal or professional,

they appreciate being active. Empower them with a role that extends beyond their traditional responsibilities. Whether it is enabling them to take part in planning the holiday party, encouraging them to take the lead on a volunteer committee, or bringing them into a leadership meeting, enabling Millennials to be involved in responsibilities that fall outside of their traditional position encourages them to remain with the company.

7. *Provide them the opportunity to give you feedback*: For some employees, lack of consistent communication with a manager drives them crazy, for others they feel they are not a priority, and still others have an inherent frustration involving managers not giving them the opportunity to prove themselves. Regardless of the pet peeve, providing Millennials the opportunity to give feedback to their manager will enable these frustrations to be discussed and for behavior to be modified (if appropriate). Rather than just asking for feedback at random times, create a set schedule that provides employees a recurrent opportunity to share what is working well and what could be improved.

8. *Communicate impending changes*: No one wants to be blindsided by a change they didn't see coming. Though leadership could be fully aware of an important change that will be taking place, employees beneath them may lack access to the same information. While most leaders do not typically mean to hide information from employees, the lack of transparency creates a barrier between the two. This disconnect naturally pushes the employee away from the company. Conversely, sharing impending changes enables employees to feel valuable. Information being passed along to team members creates a connection between the employee and the organization.

9. *Provide opportunities for growth*: Having the opportunity to improve yourself and grow in an organization is incredibly empowering. Millennials are energized when they can learn new skills, master their craft, and add more value to the company. This can be accomplished numerous ways through various resources: corporate e-learning sites, YouTube, and traditional classes led by instructors all provide employees the opportunity to develop. Beyond that, on-the-job experiences such as job shadowing, mentoring, and allowing employees to work on different teams all support growth. Empower Millennials to

use these resources (and anything else they can get their hands on) to enhance their skills and grow.

10. *Be selective*: It has been said that employees join good companies and leave bad bosses. Because of this, be selective when bringing on new management. Ensure that employees are comfortable with the leader who is coming on board. Beyond just being selective with managers, filter out employees who are toxic. While no employee is a perfect match for an organization, some people possess characteristics that make them a poor fit. When this is the case, the best choice is often removing them from the organization. While it could be appealing to reassign them, do not pass on toxic employees. Employees who work closely with toxic colleagues are at risk of following their path.

FIVE REASONS MILLENNIALS QUIT AND WHAT YOU CAN DO TO STOP THEM

"Every day I go to work I am wasting my time, not using my talents, and not making the money I deserve." Right or wrong, these are the thoughts of your Millennial employees and the reasons they are leaving your company!

So what do you do?

Give them more money? Develop new business practices that are sure to create a buzz? Or yell at your frontline supervisors and threaten them with suspension if they don't do a better job of keeping their people? Or maybe you do nothing, pretend that everything is fine and that the employee turnover isn't that bad.

Fortunately, most leaders aren't passively watching employees leave their organization without attempting to do something. They are taking action! The problem is, they are taking the wrong action by focusing on perks instead of engagement activities. While perks are fun, they merely enhance an employee's appreciation of the company temporarily. They do not encourage permanent motivation, increase long-term productivity, or help employees maintain an enduring desire to deliver exceptional performance. Instead of adding perks, leaders need to transform the way their business operates. Following are five reasons your Millennials are leaving your organization and five actions you can take to stop them.

1. *They are not involved in meaningful work*: Millennials want to make a difference at their job, but they aren't provided the opportunity. Instead, they are given menial roles that deliver minimal value.

   Enable them to serve a valuable purpose: If Millennials are provided the opportunity to make an impact and understand that what they are doing matters, they are motivated to continue producing that value.

2. *Leaders put up with low performers*: Rather than have uncomfortable conversations and address employee performance issues, low performers are allowed to stay at companies while failing to meet basic expectations. These employees are dragging the organization down and putting a heavier burden on high performers.

   Get rid of low performers and recognize high performers: Get rid of those who are not producing results. Do not let low performers weigh you down: remove them from the organization. When strong performers see slackers dismissed, they realize management really is watching and knows who is delivering results. Beyond just removing employees who are not producing, reward high performers. Give them flex time, let them work from home, and provide them high-profile projects. Celebrate their success!

3. *They are micromanaged*: Micromanaging is the essence of destroying motivation. When Millennials are micromanaged, they become unproductive and lack interest in their work. When this happens, they are ready to move on.

   Empower them with autonomy: Empowering Millennials with autonomy eliminates the confines that jobs create and releases people from drudging through unfulfilling roles. Additionally, it enables Millennials to find the most efficient way to do their jobs while liberating them from redundant tasks.

4. *Leaders don't share information*: Millennials love to be in the know. Social media, smartphones, and constant contact with virtually anyone they want at any time, Millennials love having information! So, the moment we stop sharing is the moment they start becoming interested in something else.

   Be transparent and share information: By being open and sharing information, a level of trust is created that strengthens Millennials' willingness to put forth effort. This trust increases the inclination to fully commit while simultaneously reducing the desire to look for opportunities external to the company.

5. *They don't have a clear career progression plan*: Millennials are hard-working, driven employees who want to grow in their career, but they can't because no one is showing them the way. Instead, they walk blindly into their job hoping to be successful, even though they don't know what that looks like.

   Define their career path: Show Millennials the roadmap to a successful career. Explain what they are doing well, how they can improve, and what they need to do to move up in the organization on a consistent basis.

FIVE TIPS FOR MOTIVATING MELANCHOLY MILLENNIALS

One of the most difficult things to do is to light a fire in an employee who has lost interest in their work. In today's world, this is even more challenging because of the increased number of distractions that are present. Social media, smartphones, and constant contact with virtually anyone 24 hours a day increases the challenge of getting and keeping employees engaged. While inspiring speeches create motivation for some, threats of being laid off encourage others, and exciting incentive programs energize still others, in the end these efforts traditionally fail to create lasting motivation. Following are five actions you can take to motivate melancholy Millennials.

1. *Set small weekly goals*: Melancholy Millennials often feel overwhelmed. Though they want to be productive, they don't know how. Instead, they are stretched too thin or lack awareness of where to focus. To combat this issue, put in place small, manageable goals that enable the melancholy Millennial to gain positive momentum. This will instill a new sense of inspiration to produce results.

2. *Demonstrate interest in more than just the high performers and problem employees*: There are certain employees who garner all of your attention. They are either your high performers who deliver exceptional results or the problem employees who consistently suck the life out of you. Traditionally, they make up about 20% of your staff. While it is important to nurture both the shining stars and the troublemakers, it is also critical to focus on the other 80% who often get lost in the shuffle. Paying particular attention to these individuals

instead of just the high flyers and nuisances on your team is paramount to success. This "often lost" majority has the tendency to become unmotivated due to the lack of attention they receive. Put consistent effort into growing these employees.

3. *Challenge them with transparency*: Millennials traditionally enjoy showcasing their work and are often interested in being able to present what they have accomplished. Empower those who have lost interest in producing results with the opportunity to present their accomplishments at a weekly meeting in front of their peers. Though this can't be executed for every project in every situation, jumpstarting the melancholy Millennial with this initiative may instill a sense of motivation that was previously lacking. To take this a step further, if possible provide them the opportunity to present in front of senior leadership.

4. *Get rid of busywork*: Millennials hate busywork and can usually spot it a mile away. Quite often it is a primary reason Millennials become unmotivated. Busywork crushes their spirit and makes them non-committal. Even if they are suddenly thrust back into an activity that adds value, there will instinctively be a lack of internal motivation. Remove any work that does not add value.

5. *Lead by example*: A team is a reflection of leadership. As such, your words and actions must align. Though this statement is not new or pioneering, it is exceptionally relevant for Millennials who are struggling with motivation. Nothing is more of a detractor than when a leader says one thing, yet fails to follow his or her own direction. Employees (especially melancholy employees) feed off of leadership. Because of this, when managers do not follow the rules that they have set in place for others or lack an internal drive to produce results, employee motivation plummets toward a state of discontentment and indifference. In order to motivate melancholy Millennials, lead with integrity, maintain personal accountability, and strive to deliver results.

ENDNOTES

1. K. Phillips, *Employee LEAPS: Leveraging Engagement by Applying Positive Strategies* (New York: Business Expert Press, 2016), p. 175.
2. R. Power, The 12 best ways to reward employees on a budget, *Inc*, last modified February 23, 2015, https://www.inc.com/rhett-power/the-12-best-ways-to-reward-employees-on-a-budget.html.

11

Combining Generations and Producing Results

Successfully leveraging the diversity within your organization capitalizes on the unique skills of your employee base and can be both an exceptional strength and a huge differentiator. As discussed, diversity can come in many forms, including sex, race, skin color, socioeconomic status, and age. While some leaders traditionally do a good job of taking advantage of the diversity in their organizations, often times there are challenges that persist due to a failure to successfully blend talent.

This is often due to the inability of companies to effectively blend members from different age ranges into a cohesive unit. While every organization has taken steps to enrich the talent pool through diversity, generational diversity has largely gone overlooked. While in the past those who had been in the workforce for extended periods of time usually had a more prominent role than younger employees, in today's environment, age has much less to do with where an employee is on the organizational hierarchy. This creates more intermingled organizations and forces employees from different generations to work alongside one another.

This can be a challenge. Baby Boomers, Generation Xers, and Millennials have each lived through a set of different social and historical events in their formative years that have helped to shape their unique perspectives, diverse ambitions, and distinct views of the world. Because of this, each generation approaches work with a keen methodology that does not always align with other employee groups. This makes it difficult to tap into everyone's potential due to the inevitable inconsistencies that members have with other generations.

However, we all have the same interest: the opportunity to fulfill our responsibilities and add value to the company. Yet so often distractions, clutter, and a lack of congruence in how to get there get in the way. It is more about differences with ideologies and preferences than it is with individual goals and corporate objectives. Address situations holistically, taking each generation's perspective and methodology into consideration.

The six scenarios in this chapter will improve your ability to leverage the talents of everyone in your organization and help you navigate the challenges of multiple generations working together. By successfully building a bridge between each generation in your workforce, you will create a group of committed employees dedicated to supporting one another.

The six real-world issues discussed in this chapter are:

- Five reasons other generations drive Millennials crazy
- Five reasons Millennials think differently than previous generations . . . and how you can leverage this for good
- Five tips on how to balance communication preferences amongst generations
- Teamwork and collaboration: five tips on how to blend generational preferences
- Combining Millennials and Baby Boomers: five differences that you will inevitably encounter . . . and how to manage them
- Millennials managing Baby Boomers: five keys to success

FIVE REASONS OTHER GENERATIONS DRIVE MILLENNIALS CRAZY

Every generation has people that irk them, actions that cause them frustration, and experiences that send them into a frenzy. For Millennials, this is no different. Following are five specific ways other generations drive Millennials crazy.

1. *They are slow to change.* Millennials are fast moving, multitasking, hard chargers capable of changing direction quickly and efficiently. If they can find a better process, are able to simplify a current program, or discover a new way to improve a cumbersome activity, they are ready to make the change immediately. This goes against tradition and the tendencies of other generations who typically follow a certain course of action to implement change. Millennials hate this lethargic

approach and the unnecessary procedures that they perceive are only there because of an unwillingness to modify operational activities.

Millennial Preference: Instead of being content with current operations, companies should embrace an agile approach to work and value outside-of-the-box thinking to enable continuous improvement.

2. *They are unwilling to learn how to use new technology.* While Millennials are ready to dive into technological advances, other generations are slow to adopt. Whether it is because they are used to the current technology being used, lack awareness of how new applications will simplify operations, or are afraid to step out of their comfort zone, they are hesitant to try something new. Millennials don't understand this mentality. As *the* generation that has immersed themselves in technology since they were young, Millennials can't fathom the reluctance people have and why everyone isn't diving into the latest and greatest advances that come on the market.

   Millennial Preference: Empower Millennials to take the lead on technological advances that are being implemented. This will enable the company to leverage the talents and abilities of Millennials while taking advantage of the operational and financial benefits that come with the upgrades.

3. *They waste their time*: As a generation that has been labeled impatient and wanting instant gratification, it isn't surprising that Millennials hate when people waste their time. While there is nothing you can do about certain delays, when a Millennial's time is consistently wasted for irrational reasons, they become incensed; unnecessary meetings, trivial work assignments, and irrelevant operational activities that lack substance all drag Millennials down. Even insignificant discussion that does not provide value can frustrate Millennials. For example, while Millennials love context and appreciate leaders who can captivate them with an interesting narrative, they hate stories that are irrelevant or drag on for a seemingly endless amount of time.

   Millennial Preference: To ensure you maintain the interest of Millennials, do not waste their time. Remove activities that lack substance and replace them with more opportunities for them to fulfill their role or collaborate with colleagues.

4. *They try to fit in*: Like it or not, during discretionary time Millennials usually want to be around likeminded individuals who have similar interests. So, when people from other generations act differently

to try to fit in with a group of Millennials, it usually ends poorly. Situations where this occurs frequently can include technology (i.e., social media), using lingo incorrectly, and discussing the latest fashion trends. Millennials do not want to be around individuals who are acting a certain way to try to fit in. They gravitate toward people who are authentic. Ironically, Millennials will typically embrace someone who is not like them but is true to themselves over someone who is trying to fake it. A great example of this is on the TV show *The Office*. On the show, Michael Scott is an overbearing boss who does whatever he can to fit in, and his employees hate him for it. Conversely, Dwight Schrute, the stereotypical jerk who is outwardly rude to all of his colleagues but true to himself, is treated more positively (despite not being everyone's favorite person).

Millennial Preference: Be true to yourself. Even if you do not fit in with Millennials, they are more likely to gravitate toward you if you embrace your authentic self.

5. *They don't share credit*: Imagine, you work hard on a project for months; you come in early, stay late, and put forth maximum effort to deliver an exceptional product that you and your entire organization can be proud of. The day your boss hands the deliverables over to the client should be a crowning achievement filled with excitement. Unfortunately, it is actually devastating as you witness your manager take all of the credit. When colleagues fail to acknowledge the efforts Millennials make, it tears them apart.

Millennial Preference: Though it is clear every task a Millennial completes can't be celebrated, to consistently get the best out of them, recognize their efforts, especially when they deliver superior results. This encouragement motivates them to continually put forth maximum effort. Acknowledgement, even for something small, can go a long way.

FIVE REASONS MILLENNIALS THINK DIFFERENTLY THAN PREVIOUS GENERATIONS . . . AND HOW YOU CAN LEVERAGE THIS FOR GOOD

It isn't surprising that various factors shape peoples' perspectives and outlook toward many parts of life, and that diversity can be an exceptionally powerful differentiator in the workplace. While this is often accepted when dealing with sex, race, skin color, and socioeconomic status, age is rarely examined. This minimizes the ability to leverage generational diversity. This is a huge mistake.

Millennials think, act, and work differently than previous generations. Their technological prowess, philanthropic ideology, and deep desire for meaningful work make them a great resource for companies. Unfortunately, for some reason companies fail to capitalize on this, choosing instead to put Millennials in a box. This limits the value they can deliver to organizations. Following are five reasons Millennials think differently than previous generations and how you can leverage these differences for good.

1. *They grew up with technology*: Unlike Baby Boomers and Generation X, Millennials grew up with the internet, and more generally, technology. Many Millennials can't remember a time when the web wasn't a part of their everyday lives. Conversely, Baby Boomers and Generation X spent their formative years without the internet. As such, their outlook on technological advances is vastly different. Millennials possess an extreme passion for technology and are typically able to use new programs and applications without considerable training or direction.

   Recommendation: Allow Millennials to lead technological advances and provide them opportunities to mentor employees from other generations who do not have robust technological abilities.

2. *Social media, social media, social media*: Millennials are far superior with social media than any other generation in the workforce. Facebook, LinkedIn, Twitter, Snapchat, Instagram, and others are the best places to market your company's brand and expand your digital footprint. Millennials know what is hot, what is not, how to start a movement, and what actions you need to take to make something "go viral." Mastering the use of social media can be exceptionally challenging, yet due to years of experience, Millennials are able to manage it with ease.

   Recommendation: Capitalize on the expertise Millennials have with social media to boost your company's brand or image.

3. *They had more information growing up than you ever did*: With internet access at a young age, Millennials had access to more information than any other generation ever did while growing up. This access has led to the ability to look at situations in a variety of

ways. It also enables them to see how decisions affect people who are not always in the room. This encourages them to focus on matters that extend far beyond the bottom line and can be a roadmap for maintaining ethics in the face of adversity.

Recommendation: Capitalize on Millennials' ability to look at situations from various perspectives and ensuring everyone (even those not in the room) has a voice.

4. *They are confident they are ready to lead*: In many ways, Millennials have more experience, possess better skills, and have more tangible knowledge to generate value for a company at an earlier age than any previous generation. Because of this, it isn't surprising that many have an unrelenting confidence that extends far beyond what other employees in similar positions felt just a few years ago.

Recommendation: Take advantage of this confidence and challenge them with difficult work.

5. *They view work differently than you*: Employees from previous generations lived to work or focused on maintaining a quality work-life balance. For Millennials, they work to live. They aren't interested in being on the job from sunrise to sunset or balancing appropriate time in the office with their home life. While they often catch grief for this approach, it can actually be beneficial. Millennials with this mentality actively pursue completing tasks the most efficient way possible while eliminating the need to follow unnecessary rules or formalities. This bypasses the need to complete activities that do not add value or are a waste of time.

Recommendation: Leverage Millennials' passion for streamlining operations by empowering them to eliminate redundant tasks and actions that do not add value.

FIVE TIPS ON HOW TO BALANCE COMMUNICATION PREFERENCES AMONGST GENERATIONS

There is no clear-cut way to balance the various preferences employees have when it comes to communication. Regardless of the people involved, interests usually contrast considerably. Some people want face-to-face interaction as much as possible while others value written correspondence more, and still others feel video chat and IM are the easiest way to interact. This challenge is exacerbated when employees from different generations are present. Baby Boomers, Generation X, and Millennials all have different preferences when it comes to communication, so it can be difficult to know how to engage employees effectively. Following is a brief review of the communication preferences members of each generation have.

Baby Boomers: Prefer face-to-face communication, value in-person dialogue, view technological communication as impersonal.

Generation X: Prefer the medium that is easiest, value direct communication, view a blend of communication mediums as superior to using just one.

Millennials: Prefer using technology to communicate, value having the ability to communicate 24-7 via technology, view advances in technology as reducing the need for face-to-face communication.

Because of these vast differences, the ability to develop a perfect plan that everyone will like is impossible. However, effective communication amongst colleagues is necessary. Following are five tips on how to balance communication preferences amongst generations.

1. *Respect and appreciate fellow employees*: Though this is obvious, it must be established and enforced throughout the company. It is imperative for employees to maintain a sense of reverence for one another when communicating, regardless of the medium used.

2. *Use multiple mediums to communicate*: In today's fast-paced world, employees receive hundreds of emails, field dozens of phone calls, and participate in numerous meetings every day. This leads to a surplus of information that employees can't keep up with; there simply isn't enough time. With various communication preferences desired by different employees in the workplace, it becomes even more challenging to communicate successfully. To provide the best opportunity to reach every employee, use multiple mediums to convey information. For example, while a companywide email could catch the attention of some employees, others may only heed information that comes from the daily department meeting. Using various mediums to communicate will provide everyone the opportunity to receive important information.

3. *Establish expectations*: Defining what is expected from employees is an important part of balancing communication preferences. Specifically, determining how quickly employees should respond to emails, whether a phone call, face-to-face meeting, or IM is more appropriate, and when the best time to reach out to fellow colleagues for support are all subjective. Establish expectations for the team so that everyone is on the same page.

4. *Take inventory of what your employees prefer*: While general preferences for each generation can often guide you in the right direction, your employees may have interests that stray away from the norm or are altogether different. Actively engage employees to learn about their communication preferences. This will enable you to convey important information that will keep them informed and engaged.

5. *Have quarterly meetings to address issues*: To ensure communication is fluid, host quarterly meetings with an open forum so that members of each generation can openly discuss communication challenges. These meetings will enable employees to address grievances and provide the opportunity for behavior to be modified, if necessary.

TEAMWORK AND COLLABORATION: FIVE TIPS ON HOW TO BLEND GENERATIONAL PREFERENCES

Teamwork and collaboration can be tough, especially when there is more than one generation involved. When this is the case, establish effective strategies that will enable each generation to perform their best. Prior to employing these strategies, first understand the typical outlook that members of each generation have toward teamwork and collaboration. Specifically, Baby Boomers, Generation X, and Millennials all have different viewpoints on teamwork and collaboration that can stifle productivity if not managed appropriately. Following is a brief review of how each generation traditionally feels about teamwork and collaboration.

Baby Boomers: Though not always opposed to working on a team, there isn't an intrinsic desire to collaborate with others. Baby Boomers believe everyone should have specific responsibilities, and junior roles and younger generations should defer to employees who have a higher status in the company or have been in the workforce for an extended period of time.

Generation X: Generation X is comfortable working alone or in a team environment. This generation has been simultaneously self-managing and involved in team building since they were young, so are traditionally able to perform effectively in both environments.

Millennials: Millennials love coming together as a team and thrive in a collaborative environment. They appreciate teamwork and enjoy when everyone can use their talents and abilities to bring value to the organization.

With the assorted views toward teamwork, it can be challenging to blend generational preferences that enable everyone to perform their best. Following are five tips on how to blend generational preferences.

1. *Establish ground rules*: Establishing ground rules enables employees to know what to expect. Deeper than just generic ideas, ground rules should be rooted in specific strategies and actions that blended workforces should adopt. This is especially important during long projects in which team members work closely with one another for extended periods of time. Personal preferences, collaborative and individual work assignments, and prospective team-building exercises should all be addressed.

2. *Give everyone a voice*: People are inherently more interested in performing certain functions if they are involved in the development process. Empower everyone who is part of the team to be an active participant in deciding the level of team building and collaboration. Additionally, ensure the group discusses the times when collaboration will be most effective and when working independently will be best.

3. *Explain why*: It is difficult to get behind ideas when you don't know the rationale behind them. When team building or working independently must take place, take the time to explain what employees are doing and the justification behind decisions. This ensures that you will have more commitment from everyone involved.

4. *Purposely blend generations*: Employees from each generation typically appreciate being around others in their age group. While this isn't necessarily negative, it restricts the ability to blend members

of different generations into a cohesive unit unless it is facilitated intentionally. This can cause a generational divide. As stated previously, generational diversity has the potential to be extremely powerful. Employees from different generations have unique experiences, passions, and abilities, thus possess assorted skills that they can bring to the group. Blend members from different generations to ensure those who maintain expertise in certain areas have the opportunity to work with others with a different set of skills.

5. *Ensure time is managed effectively*: Millennials don't want long, drawn-out stories, Baby Boomers aren't interested in excessive team building activities, and Generation X doesn't want to be caught in the middle. Develop realistic project plans that enable each subgroup to find their sweet spot and perform their best. While this could seem fairly obvious, by being transparent and openly establishing how you will leverage everyone's strengths, you will identify the best situations to leverage teamwork and collaboration.

COMBINING MILLENNIALS AND BABY BOOMERS: FIVE DIFFERENCES THAT YOU WILL INEVITABLY ENCOUNTER . . . AND HOW TO MANAGE THEM

Conflict in the workplace is not new. It can be valuable and bring out the best in everyone in the office. However, it can also be divisive, create rivalries, and in some instances, even pit best friends against one another. Because of this, it isn't really a surprise that Baby Boomers and Millennials don't see eye-to-eye on a lot of issues, nor is it shocking that there can be vast differences in how these employees approach their work. Though these differences do not always need to be addressed, leaders should be aware that they will surface at some point. Following are five differences that you will inevitably encounter when combining Millennials and Baby Boomers. These are not the only issues that you will come across when combining Baby Boomers and Millennials, but do represent a portion of what could cause strife.

1. *Millennials want to have their job fit into their lifestyle, they are not interested in finding work-life balance*: Millennials do not want to work in the office until late at night. Though they might be willing to work 60+ hour workweeks, it isn't the way Baby Boomers are used to.

Laptops make Millennials mobile, so the need to stay at the office until the sun goes down isn't attractive. Millennials are much more interested in working long hours in the comfort of their own home. This philosophy is exponentially more appealing when there are conflicts involving personal engagements. Millennials will gladly work well into the night if they are provided the opportunity to sneak away from work to meet up with friends for an afternoon coffee, volunteer for a local charity event, or go home to take care of a sick child.

Baby Boomers will work until the sun goes down, but would prefer to leave their work at the office. Unlike Millennials who grew up with smartphones, social media, and constant contact with virtually anyone at any time, Baby Boomers didn't have to deal with late-night emails or after-hours conference calls for the majority of their careers. When they left work, they were done for the day. Most Baby Boomers want this trend to continue. While some are fine responding to emails or getting the occasional after-hours phone call, most would prefer to leave their work at the office.

2. *Millennials want regular feedback on how they are doing.* While this could be seen as needy, Millennials are actually interested in getting consistent feedback to ensure they are doing their job the most efficient way possible. This enables them to continually improve and ensures that they will be doing what is asked of them. While formal feedback is appreciated, informal discussions can be valued as much (if not more) by Millennials.

   Baby Boomers are content receiving feedback at regular intervals. While having informal conversations about performance isn't necessarily frowned upon, feedback during scheduled one-on-ones is the preferred time to engage in these discussions. This enables Baby Boomers to be prepared for open dialogue with well-formulated thoughts.

3. *Millennials are open to changing their role and experiencing new opportunities.* While previous generations were comfortable waiting for the right time (and opportunity) for advancement, Millennials are ready to make the leap immediately. This shouldn't necessarily be surprising. Many Millennials walk into jobs with strong educations, unique abilities, and tangible knowledge that can generate value for a company immediately. Because of these skills, it isn't surprising that they are brimming with confidence and eager to take on a major role in the organization.

Baby Boomers are looking to grow in their careers if it doesn't upset their personal life. Baby Boomers are content with finding a position that is commensurate with their skills and abilities, as long as it doesn't upset their life at home. While Baby Boomers are typically willing to move up, they will only do so when the position fits into their lifestyle. Though this could be seen as contentment, they don't see value in making a change to move up the corporate ladder that will cause undue hardship. This is especially true for Baby Boomers who are approaching the tail end of their career.

4. *Millennials prefer direct, succinct communication, regardless of medium.* While long, drawn-out conversation is often welcome in other generations, Millennials don't gravitate toward that. Instead, they are interested in concise information that is powerful and direct. Additionally, they are comfortable using various mediums to communicate—email, IM, text, and WebEx are all suitable methods of communication for Millennials.

Baby Boomers are more comfortable with face-to-face interaction. Though often less convenient than other forms of communication, Baby Boomers prefer in-person dialogue over email, IM, text, and WebEx. They will go to great lengths to gather together for a meeting instead of having a less formal virtual connection.

5. *Millennials love innovation and the opportunity to use technology.* For a lot of Millennials, there is nothing better than using a new technological program or changing a cumbersome manual activity into an automated process. The opportunity to use a state-of-the-art platform that has just come on the market or replace unnecessary manual effort with technology is exciting!

Baby Boomers are slow to incorporate new technology in the office. Though not always against using new applications, many Baby Boomers see the inclusion of new technology as a burden rather than a benefit. For some this is because it would require a change in process, others lack interest in learning a new program, and still others fail to appreciate the operational or financial benefits that would come with new tools. Regardless of the reason, technological advances are usually met with resistance.

By maintaining proper awareness of these issues, the opportunity to leverage each generation's unique traits enables organizations to capitalize on everyone's strengths while leaning on other employee groups to support their weaknesses. This ultimately enables generational diversity to be a differentiator for organizations. For this to occur, leaders should follow simple, yet compelling guidance. Following are five recommendations that will enable Baby Boomers and Millennials to work together more effectively.

1. *Blend skills and balance interests.* Though it would seem fairly obvious (and easy) to leverage the skills and interests of employees, it can be difficult when seemingly conflicting priorities are in play. Differences in employee ideologies and preferences could be seen as a zero-sum game that necessitates managing every employee the exact same way. By managing this way, you will inevitably marginalize at least some of your staff. Instead, blend skills and balance interests to get the best out of everyone. For example, while a great majority of Millennials love technology and appreciate the opportunity to have their work fit into their lifestyle, many Baby Boomers are hesitant to use new applications and would rather work at the office until the sun goes down than blend work-life with life at home. Instead of instinctively feeling that everyone must march to the beat of the same drum, take advantage of the diverse skills and interests of both sets of employees by being flexible with your policies and how you manage them. Allow employees to use their strengths the best way they know how.

2. *Have quarterly meetings to discuss issues.* Too many times companies have conflict in the workplace that goes unresolved because no one is willing to bring up uncomfortable issues that require discussion. This inevitably causes frustrations to fester, with people becoming more and more exasperated as issues continue to go unaddressed. To minimize the (potential) challenges between Baby Boomers and Millennials, host quarterly meetings that bring light to the biggest and/or most frequent challenges these generations have with each other. Though this will not solve all of your problems, it will enable issues to be discussed and solutions identified.

3. *Pair up Baby Boomers and Millennials.* Quite often, we are most afraid of what we do not understand. When bringing this to the workplace, there can be a considerable disparity of skills and interests between Baby Boomers and Millennials. This has the potential to create fear or discontentment, as neither generation knows exactly what to expect from the other. However, it can also generate strength. By pairing up

Baby Boomers and Millennials, you create the opportunity for both generations to acquire a better understanding of the talents and priorities of the other. This will tear down the walls of insecurity, as both will see that the other is merely trying to fulfill their responsibilities.

4. *Millennials, you are not going to transform Baby Boomers to work like you.* Most Baby Boomers have been in the workplace longer than you have been alive, so the notion that they are going to suddenly transform their methodology isn't likely. While there will inevitably be some changes that Baby Boomers are comfortable incorporating and some outliers who will conform almost completely, there will always be some pushback. Instead of trying to change Baby Boomers, embrace their work ethic, commitment, and years of institutional knowledge. This will enable you to take advantage of their decades of experience in the workplace.

5. *Baby Boomers, you are not going to transform Millennials to work like you.* Millennials see the world through a different lens than you. Focused on speed and agility, they are driven to streamline their work-life so that they have more time to enjoy life outside of work. It is impractical to believe that they will ever be comfortable with conservative processes and the status quo. Focus on bringing out their innovative ideas and outside-the-box thinking. This will enable you to take advantage of their passion for finding efficiencies.

MILLENNIALS MANAGING BABY BOOMERS: FIVE KEYS TO SUCCESS

When Baby Boomers entered the workforce, it was rare for them to manage employees who were decades older. While some may have rocketed up the corporate ladder quickly, leadership positions were typically held by employees who had been in the workforce for an extended period of time.

Times have changed.

In today's environment, many Millennials are given leadership positions in organizations much earlier in their careers. While strong skills enable high-achieving Millennials to boast of successful careers, it does not come without a price. Many Baby Boomers take offense to Millennials coming in and leading at such a young age. This can cause contention between generations, as Baby Boomers have a propensity to believe that they have put their time in and it is their turn to be in charge. To navigate this potentially uncomfortable terrain, following are five keys to success for Millennials managing Baby Boomers.

1. *Find common ground*: A huge barrier for any leader is not being able to relate to employees. This can be exponentially more difficult when dealing with more than one generation, especially when a member of the younger generation is managing older personnel. To minimize this issue, Millennial leaders must find common ground with older employees. Whether it is a favorite sports team, interest in a similar hobby, or passion for discussing current events, build rapport by finding common ground.

2. *Be open and transparent*: Baby Boomers and Millennials think differently than each other. Though individuals in these generations could have grown up in the same town (and in some cases the same house), maintained similar values, and even attended the same school, their ways of thinking and fulfilling responsibilities at work will inevitably be conflicting. This can be attributed to a variety of reasons including the era they grew up in, current stage of life, attitude toward innovation, access to information, and family dynamics, to name a few. Regardless of the reason, when Millennials are leading Baby Boomers, Baby Boomers want to be informed and provided rationale on how decisions are being made.

3. *Be patient with innovation and technological advances*: As stated previously, Millennials love getting their hands on the latest and greatest technology, and are usually able to figure out exactly how it will simplify operational activities. Conversely, Baby Boomers do not typically have the inherent ability to successfully use technological advances unless properly trained. This makes it imperative for Millennials to be patient with innovation and technology. While they may be able to pick up a new piece of equipment and effortlessly know how to use it, that is not always the case with Baby Boomers. Baby Boomers need time and proper training to process the innovative changes. Allow this to take place. Additionally, empower Baby Boomers to ask questions to clarify any confusion.

4. *Create blended teams*: To minimize challenges age differences have the potential of creating, purposely blend employees from different generations. This will build a sense of camaraderie amongst the members of the team. While there is no getting around the vast difference in

age, providing a platform in which people from different generations can all contribute to a common goal enables everyone to maintain focus on appropriate priorities. Dedication to collective objectives will replace concern over job titles and age differences.

5. *Do not try to validate your position*: Unfortunately, there will inevitably be some Baby Boomers who refuse to acknowledge that you are the leader. While they may report to you, inwardly they still display a lack of respect for you and believe that you have not earned your position. While their thinking could be for a variety of reasons, in the end it doesn't matter. You are in this role and do not need to receive acceptance from anyone. Do not try to validate your position. Instead, use your talents and abilities to perform your job, leverage the skills of your employees, and treat each member of your team with distinct value. Successfully fulfill your role by displaying quality leadership that will get the best out of everyone under your authority.

12

The Good, the Bad, and the Ugly

Myths, inaccuracies, and half-truths can run rampant when discussing Millennials. Preconceived notions regarding their thoughts, beliefs, and work ethic are often a cornerstone for a negative perspective, with this challenge being exacerbated by the habitually reckless behavior of a select few on reality TV. The ludicrous actions by a handful of Millennials in the limelight cast a negative shadow over all in this generation. Though these actions are carried out by a small percentage of Millennials, many in the business world accept it as customary for all Millennials to act with the same carelessness.

This mentality is dangerous. Valuable Millennials can be construed as ineffective or lacking drive, when they have the potential to be respected contributors. In order to sift through inaccurate beliefs, it is important to have a grounded understanding of the Millennial perspective. While there is no way to positively (or negatively) lump every person in a generation together, the ability to navigate through vague uncertainties and unchartered experiences will be improved by having a better understanding of Millennials.

The six topics in this chapter provide insight into situations that are relatively new to the workplace, are not customary for Baby Boomers or Generation X, or do not have answers that are necessarily intuitive for leaders. Though these situations are not relevant to every organization nor do the insights provided solve every acute problem companies have, they are able to help companies address issues that are often misunderstood.

The six real-world issues discussed in this chapter are:

- Five Millennial myths
- Ten mistakes leaders make managing Millennials . . . and what you can do to avoid them

139

- Five ways to get your frontline Millennial employees to care about your customers
- Five ways to spot a Millennial who is checked out . . . and how to get them back
- Five reasons Millennials love sharing information
- Five ways to leverage technology to get the best out of Millennials

FIVE MILLENNIAL MYTHS

There are various attitudes and points of view regarding Millennials in the workplace that are unattractive. While many of these perceptions could be true, for the most part they lack credibility. Instead, they are myths that have been created because of the lack of understanding a Millennial's perspective and approach toward work. Following are five Millennial myths and the truth behind the confusion.

1. *Myth #1: Millennials are lazy.*
   Truth: Millennials are interested in finding the most efficient way to do their job.
   Previous generations were OK putting in 60-hour workweeks and equated time in the office with time being productive. Millennials realize that staying busy does not necessarily mean being productive, and late nights in the office do not always convert into better results. Instead of mindlessly punching a clock and feeling good about working from daybreak to sundown, Millennials would rather fulfill their responsibilities without having to sacrifice their lifestyle. For Millennials, it isn't about the number of hours they are working; they are more focused on finding the most efficient way of doing their jobs that won't negatively affect their busy lives.
2. *Myth #2: Millennials are entitled.*
   Truth: Millennials are ambitious and want to get to the top of the mountain.
   Millennials want to lead and aren't afraid to ask for the opportunity to do so. They want challenging projects and are confident that they can complete any task that they are assigned. This is because they grew up with parents who pushed them to pursue greatness and have

seen members of their generation start and lead multibillion-dollar companies (e.g., Mark Zuckerberg). Millennials are open to accepting new challenges and are confident they will succeed when they get the opportunity.

3. *Myth #3: Millennials don't follow directions.*
   Truth: Millennials were raised to ask the question "Why?"
   In generations past, subordinates would follow a leader's orders (for better or worse) with minimal questioning. This is different in today's workplace. In many ways, Millennials are the most prepared generation coming into the workforce ever. They have more experience, education, and tangible knowledge to generate value for a company than any previous generation. Because of this, it shouldn't be surprising that they are asking the question "Why?" Their cognitive skills are looking for a better way to complete a task and they are not content with the "We have always done it that way" mentality.

4. *Myth #4: Millennials are needy.*
   Truth: Millennials want consistent feedback.
   Millennials aren't peppering you with questions to bother you: they want to make sure they are doing their job properly. This enables continuous improvement to occur and provides them the opportunity to be more valuable to the company. It also ensures that they will stay on course with every project they are involved in.

5. *Myth #5: Millennials don't view their job as a priority.*
   Truth: Millennials prefer mobile, 24-7 access.
   Millennials are highly mobile and capable of working anywhere they have an internet connection. While for previous generations it was imperative for employees to be in the office Monday through Friday from nine to five, a laptop and an internet connection make that a thing of the past. This is why Millennials are comfortable taking an extra-long coffee break in the morning and leaving work early to play in an afternoon softball game. They know that they will inevitably jump back on their laptop in the evening to complete their responsibilities. This is hard for Baby Boomers and some members of Generation X to understand. Laptops weren't mainstream when these employees were growing up. Conversely, most Millennials can't remember a life without an internet connection everywhere they go, so plugging in at an offsite location is almost second nature.

TEN MISTAKES LEADERS MAKE MANAGING MILLENNIALS . . . AND WHAT YOU CAN DO TO AVOID THEM

Every generation has little quirks that make them unique and Millennials are no different. Because of these distinct traits, the notion that we can manage them the same way we managed previous generations is untrue. We need to change how we manage Millennials. If we don't, there is a strong probability that we will lose them. Avoid these ten mistakes leaders often make when managing Millennials and you will be able to increase retention and bring out their best!

1. *Not giving credit to others.* Millennials love producing results. However, while part of their job is to make you look good, it comes with a price. They expect recognition when they fulfill their duties. Validate their efforts and give credit where credit is due.

2. *Not explaining why.* Millennials want to know why—why a task must be completed, why a training class is important, why a process must be followed. Gone are the days that employees will mindlessly follow what the leader says needs to happen, Millennials want rationale behind the decisions. If you want a Millennial to be fully immersed in what they are doing, provide rationale: explain why.

3. *Not including technology.* Millennials can't wait to get their hands on the latest and greatest technological program or computer application. They love new technology and want it in every part of their lives, including their work. Incorporate technology in the workplace as much as possible.

4. *Not recognizing exceptional performance.* Similar to giving credit to others, Millennials want to be recognized for exceptional work. Going the extra mile and delivering a superior product is more gratifying when it is recognized. If you want consistent exceptional performance from Millennials, celebrate their accomplishments.

5. *Not providing feedback.* Few things are more unsettling for Millennials than not knowing if they are doing what the boss wants them to do. Because of this, they want feedback, and lots of it. While this may seem laborious and unnecessary, providing Millennials continuous feedback enables them to be confident that they are headed down the right path.

6. *Not adapting to meet the needs of each employee.* Millennials are not a one-size-fits-all for managers. While in the past you could potentially get away with treating most employees the same, workplaces are more diverse now than ever. This diversity can be a form of strength. In order to capitalize on this strength, you must appropriately meet the needs of each employee. Find the most effective way to get the best out of everyone by adapting your leadership style to meet their needs.

7. *Not being accessible.* Leadership accessibility is a comforting factor for Millennials. When a leader is accessible, Millennials maintain a sense of security and confidence due to the inherent awareness that their leader is present and able to provide a helping hand, if necessary. Though one could believe a leader needs to be physically present to be accessible, not being present but being available via phone, Skype, or email also instills a sense of security for Millennials.

8. *Not creating a collaborative environment.* Yes, Millennials are independent and confident in their skills, but they also want a team environment. They love collaborative work environments where they can use the talents and abilities of everyone to deliver an exceptional end product.

9. *Not challenging them with difficult work.* Millennials are interested in challenging work. With a strong education and diverse experiences under their belt, they are confident they can take on any challenge you throw their way. While it is understandable that you could be hesitant to give them work that you believe is beyond their ability, their ingenuity, unique skills, and sheer determination could shock you; and if they are unable to find a way to succeed on their own, they are sure to find someone who can help (see #8).

10. *Not understanding that it isn't all about work.* While previous generations lived to work or tried to maintain a healthy work-life balance, Millennials work to live. It isn't about the number of hours they are putting in, instead it is about finding the most efficient way of doing their job that will allow them to live the lifestyle that they want. Millennials are exceptionally busy and enjoy cramming as much into their lives as possible. They aren't interested in mindlessly punching a clock or finding work-life balance, they are more focused on living life to the fullest. Do not expect them to be in the office from sunrise to sunset, instead, provide them a fluid environment where they can fulfill their responsibilities with mobile, 24-7 access.

FIVE WAYS TO GET YOUR FRONTLINE MILLENNIAL EMPLOYEES TO CARE ABOUT YOUR CUSTOMERS

Most employees are poised to do whatever they can to help customers. However, some employees seem to lack awareness that the very customers they spurn are the only reason they have a job. This can be especially true for frontline Millennial employees. For some, the very thought of providing help to a needy customer causes them frustration. To transform this mentality, following are five actions you can take to motivate frontline Millennial employees.

1. *Show them how their actions make a difference to the end user*: When Millennials feel like they are just another cog in the wheel, they become uninterested in meeting the needs of the customer. Alternatively, when they can see how their actions make a difference in the lives of end users, they are instinctively drawn toward meeting those needs. They understand their actions are an integral part of the process. Help them appreciate the importance of their role and how it makes an impact to the customer.

2. *Make them part of the solution*: Millennials don't want to just punch a clock and fulfill a certain role, they want to be immersed in their work environment and be a part of every business decision. While it isn't feasible to make everyone a part of every decision, involving Millennials in activities that extend beyond their traditional role (but still falls in line with what they do on a daily basis) encourages them to care about their job and not feel as though they are merely a means to an end. This collaborative approach creates a shared vision of how to move forward, with employees having a stronger level of commitment for meeting each customer's needs.

3. *Make an impact that extends beyond the bottom-line for the company*: For frontline Millennials, making the company an extra dollar isn't extremely gratifying. While it can feel good to make a sale, there isn't a lot of intrinsic motivation to do so. However, Millennials are socially conscious and want the organization they work for to be as well. Because of this, incorporating social campaigns that make an impact outside of the company's bottom-line encourages Millennials to put forth maximum effort. For example, donating 10% of profits to a local non-profit encourages frontline

Millennials to work hard while satisfying their internal desire to make a positive difference in the world.

4. *Allow them to see the different parts of the value chain*: Frontline Millennials are the face of the organization and often set the tone for how a company is perceived. Not surprisingly, it is rare that they truly understand this. Walk them through how everything is connected and numerous colleagues upstream are counting on them to do their job. Frontline Millennials must understand that it isn't just about making a sale to increase revenue, but rather involves them being the final piece of the puzzle.

5. *Create a collaborative mentorship program*: Managers and supervisors are often employees who have worked in the trenches and moved up the corporate ladder, with their dedication and work ethic being a staple of how they were able to build successful careers. Typically, while they lack daily interactions with customers, their fire for serving others remains intact. Create an opportunity for frontline Millennials to work with these leaders on a consistent basis by developing a mentorship program. However, instead of a traditional mentorship program, make it collaborative by allowing both parties to utilize their unique skillsets. Leaders will be able to instill a sense of pride and purpose to frontline employees while Millennials can provide recommendations on how innovation can improve operational activities.

FIVE WAYS TO SPOT A MILLENNIAL WHO IS CHECKED OUT . . . AND HOW TO GET THEM BACK

Spotting a Millennial who is engaged at work is very easy. They start work early, send you emails late at night, and always seem to have a positive outlook on what they are doing and how they add value to the company. Conversely, recognizing a Millennial who is checked out is quite different. It is often like watching a bad slasher movie. You should have noticed what was going to happen a long time ago, but you didn't want to face the reality. Unfortunately, unlike a bad slasher movie that you can rewind to spot the dramatic scenes that precede the inevitable end, there is no rewind button for Millennials who are checked out and leave your organization. Because of this, spotting Millennials who are disengaged from their work early is necessary.

Disappointedly, quite often once you identify that a Millennial is checked out, it is already too late. They have either found a new position with another company or are so far lost that they are no longer productive and you must let them go. If you are fortunate enough to recognize a Millennial is checked out in time, there are actions you can take to transform their mentality. Following are five ways to spot a Millennial who is checked out and five actions you can take to get them reengaged.

1. *They stop asking, "Why?"*: From a young age Millennials consistently asked the question "Why?" They have always been interested in learning the rationale for decisions and constantly try to find a better way to complete a task. So, when they stop inquiring about the justification behind decisions and replace the question "why" with words like, "I'll follow orders," "I'll do what I'm told," or "I'll do whatever you want me to do," there is trouble. While it might seem like these statements are them falling in line, it is actually detrimental and demonstrates their unwillingness to continue investing in the organization. They have lost interest in their role and are on their way out.

   Involve them in an assignment that falls outside of their traditional scope of responsibilities: Employees can become energized when they are involved in activities that are outside of their traditional work responsibilities. This change infuses them with energy while enabling them to see a new part of the company. Whether it is a special assignment, temporary duty, or unique training class, the opportunity to be involved in something different is valued. Though these assignments are only temporary, they provide employees the opportunity to take a break from the monotony of their traditional tasks and focus on something that can provide them fresh energy.

2. *They go from high-achievers to doing the bare minimum*: Most Millennials are still early in their careers and want to get ahead, and are not afraid to put forth exceptional effort to achieve. While not overly interested in putting in 60+ hour workweeks like their parents did, they are comfortable immersing themselves in the job. So, when a Millennial transforms from being an employee who consistently delivers extraordinary results to a "clock-watcher" who does the bare minimum, they are inevitably lacking a sense of connection to the organization and are contemplating departing.

Give them responsibility and challenge them with difficult work: Ownership and challenge breed engagement. When employees need to dig deep and put forth their best effort, they must immerse themselves in their work. Whether it is being assigned a new task, empowering them to change a certain process that needs to be updated, or giving them an additional duty (e.g., coordinating the holiday party), providing them increased responsibility and challenging work has the potential to reinvigorate them.

3. *They display a disregard for their work and your approval*: Millennials take pride in their work and appreciate being recognized by superiors for their efforts. So, when a Millennial displays an outward disregard for the job (i.e., playing on their phone in a meeting, surfing the web, texting with friends, etc.) and are not trying to hide it from their manager, it is clear they are no longer invested.

    Find them a new role: Quite often, employees who are checked out are on the verge of leaving the company. When this is the case, drastic measures are often necessary. Pulling the employee from their current role and moving them to a new position in the organization could benefit everyone involved and may instill a new sense of motivation for the employee.

4. *They suddenly become quiet*: Engaged employees, especially Millennials, are usually vocal while maintaining a palpable zest for the organization. So, when your most passionate Millennials suddenly become quiet and indifferent, you are at risk of losing them.

    Take them out of their current work environment: Similar circumstances typically generate similar results. When dealing with a Millennial who is checked out, this can be troublesome. How is a disengaged employee supposed to change their mentality if they are stuck in the same environment that depletes them of energy and pushes them away from wanting to do work? Change their environment by moving them to a new location in the office or connecting them with new members of the team. This will generate new energy.

5. *They show no signs of interest*: Most Millennials, whether it is formal or informal, enjoy getting involved in their work environment—this could include being on a committee, hosting an event, or serving food at the holiday party. Regardless of the activity, they appreciate the opportunity to take an active role in the organization. So, when a Millennial shows indifference to extracurricular activities at work and displays no interest in participating, they are likely checked out.

Allow them to work on a pet project: Everyone has pet projects that they would like to work on and have hidden passions that surface every now and again. To reignite the passion in Millennials who are checked out, it may be beneficial to allow them to work on a pet project that will restart their engine. Though not an activity you can implement all the time, providing the opportunity for Millennials who are checked out to pursue a pet project could be just what is needed to reengage them.

FIVE REASONS MILLENNIALS LOVE SHARING INFORMATION

Generations have vastly different perspectives involving what information they should share. This can lead to considerable challenges due to each generation maintaining allegiance to practices that do not always align with other subsets of the workforce and has the potential to alienate others. When dealing with Millennials, this can be a problem. It is no secret that Millennials love sharing information. This can cause issue with other generations due to their lack of understanding why. Following are five reasons Millennials love sharing information.

1. *Transparency promotes trust*: Proactively sharing information on a consistent basis enables companies (and leaders) to build social capital with employees. This trust reduces members' willingness to believe unconfirmed gossip and the inclination to second-guess the motives of the organization knowing that they have previously been forthright. Most Millennials have a huge fear of missing out, and if open discussion does not occur frequently, can believe that they aren't being provided important information.

2. *Transparency strengthens teamwork and unity*: Sharing information levels the playing field, which inevitably builds rapport and boosts mutual respect. As members of an organization consistently pass information back and forth, focus shifts toward work and away from rank and job title. The mission of the company becomes the priority.[1]

3. *Transparency reduces duplication of work*: Cross-functional projects and interdepartmental coordination are commonplace in the business world and critical to success. By failing to share information

and discuss operational activities, duplication of work can be rampant. Conversely, by opening up the lines of communication, synergies are discovered and the ability to eliminate redundant operations can occur.[2]

4. *Transparency eliminates the spreading of rumors*: Just as it was 50 years ago, water cooler discussions generate enticing information. This leads to half-truths and mixed rumors that have the potential to stifle productivity and create conflict. By sharing information, the rumor mill will be quieted. Accurate information will replace false claims.

5. *Transparency holds people accountable*: Fabricated stories have long been a part of the workforce. Many employees instinctively stretch the truth to make it seem as though they have completed part of a project or delivered their portion of work, when, in reality they are merely passing it on to someone else. By sharing information, the ability to do this is minimized. Employees can no longer hide behind ambiguity and blamelessness. Instead, they are held accountable for their actions. Everyone will know who is responsible for each task and what has been accomplished.

FIVE WAYS TO LEVERAGE TECHNOLOGY TO GET THE BEST OUT OF MILLENNIALS

Most Millennials can't wait to get their hands on the latest and greatest technology on the market. They are drawn to the newest applications and hottest social media platforms, and are excited to immerse themselves in the next big thing. Sometimes their excitement is so palpable that they lose track of everything else around them; they are simply captivated by their new toy. Traditionally, this far exceeds the interest of Baby Boomers and Generation X. While members of these generations could have a general interest in new technology, it pales in comparison to a Millennial's drive.

However, while Millennials can (and often do) incorporate as many technological advances as their heart desires in their personal lives, professionally, technological upgrades do not occur as often. Nonetheless, Millennials want to use new technological products, applications, and services as much as possible. Following are five ways to successfully leverage Millennials' interest in technology.

1. *Make sure Millennials are part of any pilot program involving new technology*: Because Millennials are drawn to technological advances, it is natural to include them on the piloting of new programs. While it is not advised (or even feasible) to have every Millennial be a part of the team that tests new technology, leveraging this generation's interest in technology by having subsets serve as testers will take advantage of their technological prowess.

2. *Allow Millennials to work from home at least once a week*: For some companies, this is not a stretch. Yet for others, this goes against company policy that is steeped in tradition. While maintaining strong traditions is admirable, the only certainty in business is change. When appropriate (and possible), many companies now allow at least some form of telecommuting for their employees. Regardless of the rationale for allowing employees to work from home, it is exceptionally appealing for most in this generation. Millennials would rather work in the comfort of their own home (or coffee shop down the street), than trudge into the office. Though not feasible for every company or role, if possible, provide Millennials the opportunity to take advantage of fulfilling their duties outside of the workplace on a consistent basis.

3. *Challenge Millennials to teach older generations how to use new technology*: Technology is great, if you are able to use it. Unfortunately, while some people have a knack for seamlessly picking up and using new programs and applications, others invariably fail to successfully use technological advances correctly. Instead they are stuck on the sidelines while growing increasingly hesitant to adapt their current activities and methodology. This is disconcerting. For companies to flourish, employees from every generation must be able to successfully use new programs and applications that the company adopts. Empower Millennials (especially those who are drawn to new technology) to teach colleagues how to use new programs and applications.

4. *Challenge Millennials to write a report about the pros and cons of adding a new piece of technology*: For some Millennials, every program and application is vital to the success of the organization; without the latest and greatest technology, the company will inevitably fall behind the competition, lose market share, and go out of business. In reality, it is very unlikely that such grand changes will materialize from not getting a single piece of equipment or software. However, rather than

snuff out an idea without due process, challenge the employee(s) who are interested in getting the new technology to justify the addition. More than just information taken from the website, provide them the opportunity to create a report highlighting the pros and cons of acquiring the new technology. This will require them to defend their position while simultaneously developing important management skills that will serve them well as they grow with the company.

5. *Challenge Millennials to do a cost/benefit analysis*: Similar to challenging Millennials to write a report, require them to do a cost/benefit analysis regarding why a certain piece of technology is worth purchasing. Millennials often fail to incorporate the financial implications of a new product into their thought process. By challenging them to do a cost/benefit analysis, they will be required to make decisions that extend beyond just adding a new tool. They will be forced to assess the financial burden the purchase will have on the company.

ENDNOTES

[1] K. Phillips, *Employee LEAPS: Leveraging Engagement by Applying Positive Strategies* (New York: Business Expert Press, 2016), p. 56.

[2] W. Johnson, 4 benefits of sharing information in the workplace, *Small Business Trends*, last modified January 25, 2017, https://smallbiztrends.com/2017/01/benefits-of-sharing-information-in-the-workplace.html.

Conclusion

While it is important to have a strong strategy, superior products, and the financial means to execute, failure to implement change in the workplace will lead to reduced productivity and increased turnover. Unfortunately, change is difficult and can often be scary. This pushes many leaders away from wanting to transform operational activities or cater to a specific subset of the workforce. However, change is necessary to succeed.

Success will always hinge on the ability to take advantage of changes in the workplace. This does not happen by accident—hard work, dedication, and the continual pursuit of managing the simultaneous changes in the business world and workforce is necessary. This is done through modifying management practices and instilling progressive leadership concepts. Though reading this book will help you better understand Millennials, and the specific actions shared can empower you to improve operations, minimal benefits will emerge without taking the next step.

You must take action!

Use the guidance and direction provided in this book. This will enable you to formulate a strategy that is focused on increasing productivity and profitability. The power to motivate Millennials and turn potential into productivity is in your hands. Use *Managing Millennials* to transform your organization and take it to the next level.

Index

Note: Page numbers in italic and bold refer to figures and tables respectively.